Books by Louise de Kiriline Lawrence

THE LOVELY AND THE WILD

A COMPARATIVE LIFE HISTORY STUDY
OF FOUR SPECIES OF WOODPECKERS

THE LOGHOUSE NEST

THE QUINTUPLETS' FIRST YEAR

Louise de Kiriline Lawrence

THE LOVELY AND THE WILD

Drawings by Glen Loates

McGRAW-HILL RYERSON LIMITED

Toronto   Montreal   New York   London   Sydney
Johannesburg   Mexico   Panama   Düsseldorf
Singapore   Rio de Janeiro   Kuala Lumpur   New Delhi

ISBN 77445-3

Library of Congress Catalog Card Number: 68-20508

Printed and bound in Canada

2 3 4 5 6 7 8 9 10 HR   0 9 8 7 6 5 4 3

To M. M. N.

Contents

One

This Was the Beginning

The young child in the carriage looked up into the blue sky as a pair of hooded crows flew over, cawing.

The child's eyes followed the crows.

"Kraa, kraa, kraa," she pronounced softly and smiled as if in recognition of the link between the birds and the sound.

I can remember nothing of this, of course. But my mother loved to tell this story of her daughter's first sign of awakening awareness directed, not to the usual objects of baby talk, mummy and daddy, but to birds, creatures of nature. And whatever bearing this may or may not have had upon this child's future preoccupations, it was, nevertheless, linked with the whole atmosphere of my home and childhood in Sweden.

When my father married he built for himself and Mother a separate home in splendid seclusion about a mile from the Big House and other buildings of our estate Svensksund. Here we lived until Grandfather's death. After that Father took full possession of the estate and we moved from Villan to the main residence.

Father's choice of the location for his villa was characteristic. The brown-stained house, its roof peaked high to defeat the burdens of heavy snow in the winter, was placed atop the rounded head of a granite bluff. Voluminous spruces that sang in the wind surrounded it, and tall pines whose tufted branches, collected all at the top of the trees, looked like hats mounted on the pylonlike red trunks.

From this pinnacle the land falls away on all sides, and in whatever direction one elects to look the view is magnificent. To the south and west a country of squared fields, dotted with woodlots and toy-sized houses, spreads beyond a wide opening in the villa forest for miles to the distant horizon. To the north, seen from Father's graveled terrace high above the tops of the trees which grow at the foot of the bluff and climb up its sides, opens a panoramic vista of land and water.

To my dying day I shall never forget this view from the villa terrace with light and shadow playing upon the Nordic landscape. For there I was born and to this land I belong forever. The sky, arched and free, the water spreading in tongues and strips between dark-green wooded islets and promontories, blend with each other in the mood conjured by the current moment. This is the fjord of Bråviken that cuts deep into the east coast of Sweden from the Baltic Sea. On its north shore cliffs rise abruptly to shape the bulwark of the Kolmården forest, a forest tall, dark, and mysterious, ripe with legendary sagas from former centuries of highwaymen and brigands. In the midst of the blue-green part of the forest exposed to our view is a conspicuous landmark shining chalk-white, a large quarry where the beautiful green-veined Kolmård marble has been mined for centuries in the past.

The south shore of Bråviken is scooped out into a wide bay of smooth water dotted with grassy and wooded islets. On each of the bay's three sides the white and buff-colored walls and the tall windows of dignified century-old manor houses peek forth amid lush verdure. The Big House of Svensksund and Father's villa crown the bay's west side.

The shore on the Svensksund side is edged with swaying reed beds that grow out into the shallow water. Crested grebes, ducks, and other waterfowl find here a ready retreat and abundant material for their secretive nestings. A strip of wet meadow half a mile wide, full of tussocks and puddles, runs along the whole shoreline. Once upon a time the sea washed over it to the foot of the granite rock. This meadow is ideal shorebird habitat, and in the spring a vast assortment of ruffs, lapwings, snipes, and sandpipers arrive to display, to nest, and to raise their young during the brief northern breeding season on this 58th parallel. And they fill the place with shrill calls, with movement and great excitement.

The lapwings etched themselves most deeply upon my memory, these beautiful birds with their black fronts and iridescent backs, and their spectacular crests curving over their foreheads and crowns to a long upswept end. Even today I can hear their plaintive cries, *vee-weep—vee-weep—vee-weep*, as I did when I ran barefoot over the tussocks and saw them rise upon rounded wings in defense of eggs and young. Once I found an egg, carried it home, and put it in Mother's incubator to hatch. In my childish ignorance I did not realize, of course, that this was to commit sacrilege against nature's good order and purpose, since my own purpose was little else than random curiosity. When Father found out he soon stopped any further egg thefts.

The path from the meadow zigzags up a steep incline to another terrace where sprawls the Big House amid close-cropped lawns. It is a large homey-looking house. A number of irregular wings jut out from its main body, each representing an addition built in the course of time to accommodate the successive families. The walls of the house disappear beneath a thick covering of Virginia creepers that garland the windows, and climbing honeysuckle at blossom time spreads its heady perfume through every open window. The roof laid with wavy tiles of red brick emerges with difficulty from all this clinging viridescence.

As a centerpiece in the middle of the circular driveway in front of the house a hawthorn of gargantuan dimensions once grew in splendid isolation. So long as I can remember it never missed bursting into bloom four days before midsummer, on the night before my young sister's birthday. She awakened and looked out and there it stood, a matchless decoration to celebrate such a day, decked with a million miniature pink roselike blossoms.

Two mute swans lived in a pond whose dark surface reflected the south side of the house, and a pair of peacocks strutted importantly along the terrace under a row of horse-chestnut trees. Gnarled with age and enormous of girth, indicating a lifetime of no less than three hundred years, these venerable trees framed the same view over the fjord as seen from the ramparts of Villan, and their pendulous branches swept the gravel of the terrace when the wind blew from the sea. Who planted these ancient trees that must have been there even when the enemy burned and sacked the estate during the wars of the eighteenth century? The unwritten history of Svensksund does not tell. And if the planter as he tenderly adjusted the saplings' roots in the good earth did not dream they would survive through such a lengthy period of time, he must have had a vivid idea of creating an enduring treasure to be cherished by himself and passed on to posterity. Such is the worship of trees.

I was nine years old when we moved to the Big House. Before this event my impressions of the natural environment, the villa forest, the little dell where the blueberries grew, the rocky shelves of granite where my sister and I used to play house, were limited to an idea of having a native connection with all this simply because I was born there. I belonged to the surroundings and consequently was one with them.

Life at the Big House changed this. There I also became the

observer. Many things contributed to this change, but chief among them was the influence of my father. Naturally I adopted his views and attitudes quite uncritically, just because they were his. Later, of course, the process of experience sifted some of this away as chaff and other parts were moderated to fit more advanced ideas. But to this day one adage of his remains particularly clear and fast: "Be never afraid!" And by this he meant, as I now understand, every kind of fear.

Father was a keen hunter and his ideas about nature conservation were quite naturally colored by this circumstance. For instance, he felt strongly that all animals that he considered detrimental to the crops and to the hunter's "rights" must be outlawed and suppressed, if not annihilated. There was no other way and it is strange how badly this fitted with the rest of his conceptions about nature. Among the animals that earned his disapproval were the domestic cat, justifiably so if allowed to roam without restraint, the ubiquitous house sparrow, crows, rats, and the beautiful large red squirrel of northern Europe. When I became big enough to handle a small gun with some responsibility, Father enlisted me as assistant pest controller and paid me a bounty for every rat's tail or pair of sparrow's legs, items that appeared most frequently on my list of "game."

For the benefit of the Svensksund hunting, which had a reputation to maintain, Father raised ring-necked pheasants. Although these birds were not native to this northerly region, they were easily acclimatized. Eggs were hatched under hens that lived in little cages in a field between Villan and the Big House, and at a safe age the young pheasants were liberated into the landscape. Father and his huntsman, a special retainer who did nothing but train Father's hounds, care for the pheasants, and carry the bag during the hunting season, watched over the game birds with the utmost solicitude. The success of each year's "crop" was of much concern to Father and the "yield" of his reserved hunting grounds a matter of pride.

Hunting in northern Europe was then and probably still is

conducted along the same lines as it is now on the game farms in North America. If there is any advantage in such practices, maybe it lies in the suppression of ruthlessness and in the encouragement of a greater sense of responsibility necessary to maintain profitable game-farm hunting. This can hardly be achieved in the heat of strong competition over decreasing game when throngs of hunters during the open season gain practically free admission everywhere to slay, often wantonly, all that moves within range of their guns. Whichever method may be considered most desirable from the sportsman's viewpoint, with Father one thing was of paramount importance. This was a set of ethics, also called sportsmanship. I never saw Father aim at a sitting duck or a motionless animal. I never knew him take advantage of any situation in which the game had not a fair chance of escape. The bag never seemed to be to him of overriding importance.

I remember being allowed to come with him of a late afternoon and running breathlessly beside the tall blond man, trying to keep up with his seven-league stride, until we got to the escarpment at the edge of the villa forest over which the ducks flew inland for their evening feed in the fields. We would crouch there between two rocks and I would witness his skill and subdued excitement over the sporting shot at one of these birds whizzing past overhead. He was a fast and an accurate shot. I can remember his elation over the beauty of the situation as he stood on the ready watching for the rise of a covey of partridges on whirring wings in front of the motionless pointer's nose, an elation stirred to a high pitch by the effort leading up to it rather than the expectation to kill, the trudging, tramping over the wide open fields, the smell of the soil underfoot, the soft sunshine, the transparency of the air so close to the sea.

Perhaps now, so many years later, I am apt to idealize him. Truth is often revealed by hindsight and, looking back, I realize much better the depth and the quality of his feelings. For it was this kind of sensitivity that was at the bottom of Father's adoration of nature. His whole being was enwrapped in it. He could not have lived in a place where he was not in the closest contact with it. He loved all of it, the wee *tussilagos* (coltsfoot) that in the early spring pushed their heads through the wet clay and opened their sunshiny faces all along the water-filled ditches of the snow-soggy fields; the white anemones that like a thick snowy carpet spread over the brown leaves dropped last autumn from Grandmother's plantation of larch trees on each side of the road to Villan. He taught me to watch for the skylark's first ecstatic flight-song into the blue in late February. He enjoined me to check the arrival of the pied wagtail under the great maple tree precisely on the eighth day of April, and it was never late. From his suggestion that it sounded like the pronunciation of the name of a famous regiment, I learned the phonetics of the song of the chaffinch. And with his help I discovered one day the elusive corn crake by its raspy utterance out in the hayfield in the days when this bird was still plentiful.

In the winter Father arranged a feeding place for the birds outside the drawing-room windows. The food consisted of seeds, millet, hemp, mixed with rendered congealed fat. The mixture was molded in earthen flowerpots, turned out, and then strung on strings in a long row. He also had several large sheaves of corn erected on posts on the front lawn. The birds clung to the sheaves and busily husked the corn. What fell on the ground was soon picked up by an elegant pheasant cock or his demure companion as with dignity and assurance they stepped from cover once the season of deadly pursuit had ended.

Here at the drawing-room window I did my first bird-watching. I learned to know the self-important great tit and the perky blue tit from the scarlet-chested bullfinches. I hung in the window and watched the birds with ever-growing fascination.

And it was here that I first knew the excitement of spotting a rarity, when the crested tit once in a long while elected to appear and mingle with the gay crowds of common birds.

The transmission of his own delights to me was the result of only a part of Father's preoccupation with the things of nature. The influence of his enthusiasm and his observations spread much further into the society of men of art and science. To theirs he added his own contributions; and soon, the ties between them having already been forged during the years of study at the University of Uppsala, he was included in the elite group of his contemporaries famous for their devotion to the natural sciences and the protection of nature and its resources.

One day while we were still living in Villan, we watched with surprise the uncommon sight of a man walking around the

bend of the road and up toward the house. Nobody ever came on foot. Visitors arrived in carriages drawn by snorting horses, dashing up the hill and with an elegant sweep around the rock garden coming to a halt in front of the door. But this stranger, who was he?

I remember him today as if it were only yesterday I gazed upon him with the questioning curiosity of a child. Thickset and powerfully built, he walked slowly with a slightly slouching gait. His cheeks were of the healthy tint common in men of the out-of-doors, his mouth half hidden by a limp moustache. His sharp steel-blue eyes looked penetratingly and far, as if used to finding the most interesting sights in the distance. It was Bruno Liljefors, Father's friend, one of the world's finest painters of birds and nature.

No sentimentality troubles Bruno Liljefors' paintings. They depict intense action, often the dramatics of stark predation, feathers flying, the blooded tooth and nail, in honest recognition of nature's intrinsic character, her sovereign prerogative over her lesser children. Often they represent action poised at the instant of a still uncertain outcome. For example, the golden eagle's attack on a running hare is composed with such masterly skill that it is impossible to foretell whether or not the hare escapes by a hair's breadth the heavy shadow that suddenly falls upon it from above.

And yet in others of his paintings and in the details of the background his sensitivity of technique, his appreciation of color and light effects, create the brooding peace of forest and field of an order very seldom reproduced. I recall especially one picture of a hare running leisurely through the morning mist across an open field; another of a small flock of whooper swans coming down for a landing at the edge of the sea against the backdrop of a horizon softly illuminated by a sun already set; and still another of a female merganser swimming on a glazed pool in the dim eerie light of the northern night, caught by the master's brush just as she engulfs a gleaming fish head first. The artist must have seen with his own eyes these scenes and innumerable other rare incidents which are so often beyond imagination and which his enormously rich artistic output proclaims with such flawless conviction.

Liljefors stayed with us overnight and he and Father talked. What impressed my childish mind was not what they said—for I remember nothing of this—but the intensity of expression upon their faces and the seriousness of their voices as they discussed important things. The next day Father took his guest to the yard where the pheasants were kept and presented him with a pair. And Liljefors left.

Several months later the mail brought Father a package. It contained a canvas depicting a hen pheasant crouching against a tussock of dead grass with which her brown-speckled plumage blends so perfectly that she can hardly be seen. Beyond and a little ahead of her under the low green branch of a young spruce stands the resplendent cock, alert, watchful, his long barred tail half hidden in the grass. The picture was signed: "To my friend Sixten Sixtenson Flach. Bruno Liljefors 1904."

Another memory, rather dim, relates to a visit some years later of the already famed ornithologist Einar Lönnberg. I know practically nothing of his work except that I often find present-day ornithologists referring to his writings. But then I saw him in real life and I remember that in looks he was the same type as Liljefors, a fair man of goodly dimensions with a walrus moustache.

He stayed with us several days. The greatest part of this time he and Father were to be found in the smoking room on the second floor. Deeply ensconced in easy chairs by the window overlooking the pond of the mute swans at the back of the Big House, a large moose hide spread under their feet, and blue smoke circling from pipe and cigar, the two discussed the waterfowl situation around Bråviken and along the Baltic coast. And as I listened, sitting on the moose hide, for the first time in my life I became dimly aware of nature as something very real

and very important, something of an encompassing world within which our lives are not only shaped and molded but wherein
responsibilites exist for us to fulfill. This Father and his friend
Einar Lönnberg were trying to work out as they sat there absorbed in their discussions. If our role is to manage—I can almost imagine them using the very words—then our management should be one based on devotion and respect, on knowledge and wisdom.

It was inevitable that growing up in this atmosphere and being influenced by Father's ideas of what is worthwhile, his love
of nature, and his sense of strong kinship with the land should
leave a marked imprint upon my own aims and values in later
life. Had Father's influence been allowed to continue, his land
would eventually have been mine and I would never have left
it. His untimely death when I was seventeen crashed like a
thunderbolt into my life, tearing its groundworks asunder. It
flung us away from the land and into the maelstrom of city
living. What happened after this during the twenty-five years
that elapsed before once again I acquired close ties with a piece
of land to call my own, this time on the other side of the globe,
is a long and shifting story that does not belong to this book.

CHAPTER TWO

A Piece of Land

Hidden in wonder and snow, or sudden with summer,
This land stares at the sun in a huge silence
Endlessly repeating something we cannot hear. Inarticulate, arctic,
Not written on by history, empty as paper,
It leans away from the world with songs in its lakes
Older than love, and lost in the miles.

—F. R. SCOTT, *Selected Poems*

The loss of Svensksund left me with a dream, nothing else, a dream of a piece of land where once again I could live and take root. The sense of kinship with the earth and the land is a true and sound one and whosoever withdraws from it is apt to lose therewith part of his vital ballast.

The dream pursued me as an ache. It was often submerged by the pressing demands of the moment, but it always resurged with never-failing buoyancy. And in the course of the years, in the grind of the search, it became whittled down, as might be expected, to mere essentials. Nevertheless, it remained a worthwhile vision. Sun, water, and trees, nature unadulterated, these were the principal prerequisites. Included was also a bit of space to move in and to live with, to call our own, into which no man could come uninvited. There was to be a house emerging from and designed in harmony with its setting and background. In this house life was to be simple, unsophisticated, dealing directly with things that are real and authentic.

Dreams do not often come true, but mine did thirty years ago. The end of the long search always carries with it an element of surprise. It seems unbelievable. And it is unbelievable —not that the realization of the dream should lack part of the original ingredients, but that the reality is acceptable without them. Almost unaccountably all the parts of my dream fell together, one by one. My own part was to recognize the form that the dream took eventually, to grasp the opportunity when it came without hesitation, without looking back. This was perhaps a daring act prompted by intuition, little else, and almost totally lacking any premeditated assurance of success, financially or otherwise. It was like stepping through Alice's looking glass into an unknown and fantastic world whose limits were nowhere and of whose conditions and demands we, my husband Len and I, realized practically nothing. But, of course, this is the ephemeral stuff of which dreams are traditionally made.

So there we were, and there was the land, surveyed and bought, waiting for the house to be built upon it. By no standards could the land be called exceptional, not even in the overall quality of its beauty. There are pieces of land ten times more beautiful and vastly superior in every other respect. There are houses bigger and better, altogether incomparable to the one we planned on a very limited budget, on the scale of a snail's house as likened to a palace. That is from the superficial standpoint which leaves out the vital aspects. There are things that are far more important about a piece of land, that reach deep down into its past, revealing its present and indicating the promise of its future, that unveil its most secret and profound essence and beauty unrivaled by anything else anywhere else.

To start with we knew as little of all this as the casual visitor does. We could only surmise that the land contained more of beauty and value than it disclosed to the superficial glance. We were prepared to stay and to let the land unfold its saga in its own good time. With or without us and ours, this land, apart and by itself, we recognized as the foundation and the substance of a continuing epic, constantly shifting in content and outcome, to be lived and relived each passing year, a story divided into endless chapters containing minutes, hours, days, years, and eons, dealing with life in myriad forms, some supplanting each other as ecological changes occur, all with their being enmeshed within one another as an intricate puzzle-work. Into the midst of this space, this limited area, we transplanted ourselves without invitation. We found that it contained within itself territory upon territory, spread out side by side or superimposed upon one another, all belonging to this vast aggregate of living creatures. All these together, in their most primitive as well as their more advanced forms, had already evolved among themselves a relatively harmonious state of existence, based upon a curiously relevant enforcement of tolerance. Our willingness to read the signatures of nature and our readiness to live with eyes and ears open and receptive—the open mind came only much later—proved to be our best passport into this exclusive community.

The land through which the Mattawa River flows is among the oldest on earth. Its bedrock belongs to the Pre-Cambrian or Canadian shield. According to the geologists, this region lies within the so-called Grenville province whose rocks are metamorphic, which means changed in form, "born of fire." [1] Hence what we see today of these rocks in the rounded hill, in the abrupt natural rockcuts sheared through the landscape here and there to form unexpected canyons, in the crystalline pink feldspar and white quartz coming to light in veins running southwest to northeast in odd and secretive places, gives ample and dramatic evidence of the molten substances that cooled into firmness some five hundred million years ago and imprinted this scene with its unique character.

Innumerable signs record the effects of water upon the rock. Once, perhaps not so long ago, this river flowed high and

[1] Walter M. Towell, 1964, *A Naturalist's Guide to Ontario*, University of Toronto Press, p. 3.

broad, spilling its abundant volume of water into depressions long since gone dry. But as the land rose and the water level sank and the river wore itself deeper into the rock, parts of the river bed became exposed. Where former eddies swirled, now nests of rounded and oval-shaped boulders, worn smooth by the age-long grinding process of water and ice, are laid bare. Indeed, the rocks and boulders collected and dropped by the moving glaciers that covered this continent during the last ice age, some of them buried under millennial deposits of sandy loam, others piled high in elongated drumlins, are the theme of this land. Along the ancient river bed potholes of all sizes from teacups to enormous cauldrons are gouged into the rock by the frantic, wearing dance of stones and pebbles trapped inescapably in some primordial hollow and powered by the gushing waters; and today, eloquently attesting the rise of the land, most of these potholes are found high and dry, sometimes at the top of the cliffs. In other places where in times past the passage between the cliffs narrowed, the impatient force of the water tore loose huge fragments of rock; and there where once they were tossed and upended, these giant blocks still stand today adorned with mutlicolored lichens.

The Mattawa River is born from the overflow of Trout Lake, twenty miles west of Pimisi Bay. Passing through a number of smaller lakes, it gathers on the way a considerable volume of water, which pours in a thundering fall over the lip of Lake Talon. Below the falls, through a widening gorge half a mile long, the swollen river wells into Pimisi Bay with the foam from the chute still riding atop its black surface in a fantastic marbled pattern.

The sheer rocky walls of the gorge provide this rugged landscape with its most dramatic effects. Seeds whirled over the precipice from the forest that crowns the brow of the cliffs take precarious foothold in minimal deposits of soil and then miraculously produce creeping clawing upside-down versions of the parent plants. Spawning eels flipping onto the lower

ledges along the water line in high excitement are sometimes helplessly stranded there to be devoured by black bears just out of hibernation. The fleet deer sprinting at high speed away from pursuing timber wolves trips over the treacherous edge of the cliff and falls to its death below. But here, too, over these cliffs coal-black ravens with ragged wings perform their courtship flights to the accompaniment of ravenish songs, weird to the ear of man, and on a narrow ledge a hundred feet above the river they refurbish their old nest, lay their eggs, and hatch their young before spring has time to turn into summer. Paradoxically, these rough cliffs also provide a sweetly benign environment for the rarest of cliff-climbing ferns in these parts, the slender cliff brake, which here reaches its northernmost limit, and for the seasonal parade of saxifrage, columbine, and harebell, each of which in its own good time successively paints the russet rock with its specific color, white, then red, then blue.

Over the whole of the Canadian shield, lakes and ponds linked by rivers and creeks dot the landscape and act as valves in a vein, holding back the water on its way from the height of the land to the sea. Pimisi Bay is such a reservoir of water where the river slows down temporarily, spreads out, and wets the land and the air with its humidity. Here the word is to linger. But the river knows no rest. As it leaves Pimisi Bay, it runs in twists and turns through the lonesome uninhabited country of the northwest end of the Laurentian range, gurgling and splashing in a series of white water and minor cataracts, until finally, fifteen miles farther on, in a splendid scenic confluence it gives itself up to the Ottawa River.

This is historic ground. It is part of the Great Waterway that crosses this immense land. By way of four divides where the distances between the headwaters of the rivers running east, west, north, and south are measurable by mere miles or even paces, without a single connecting canal dug by man, it links ocean with ocean. Nowhere else upon this earth has a natural communication system been designed on such a grandiose scale.

Except for the inordinately slow process of soil creation and land erosion, time has wrought little change in the Pimisi Bay and Mattawa River country since the retreat of the last glacier. The forest still grows thick for miles inland. These paths over which we carry our canoes today the red man began to use with only minor alterations soon after the retreat of the ice

ten thousand years ago. With man's utilization of these trails our lake came to assume special importance. Whether he paddles up stream or down, the traveler of the Great Waterway, past or present, arrives at Pimisi Bay toward the end of the day. Behind him in whichever direction he came are long hours of exhausting effort. The trail has taken him through incredibly

rough and craggy terrain, up and down through deep rocky ravines, through swamps and forest filled with dense undergrowth and strewn with windfalls. East of Pimisi Bay a succession of difficult portages, especially the one around Paresseux Falls, has worn him out, and if he came from the west he has just conquered the portage at Talon Chute known as the most formidable for its length on the whole route from the St. Lawrence to the Great Lakes.

But here is the quiet water of Pimisi Bay, and its north shore is sheltered from the north wind by a semicircle of tall forest that seems to embrace and to hold for him the warmth of the setting sun and the peace and relaxation he needs after his laborious day. So the voyageur beaches his canoe: I rest over here! And I am told that this is exactly what *Pimisi* means in the Indian dialect from which the word comes. And here the traveler rests today as he did throughout the ages of the past.

Then came the white man. From now on the watchword was fur, and again fur, to satisfy the whims and vanities of an older and sophisticated community of men across the seas, fur traded from a population of hunters and extracted from the hunted that had hitherto lived and died together in decent innocence and in a kind of compensating harmony in the vastness of an as yet unknown and unmapped continent. With the pressure of demand upon them, the preserving elements of innocence and harmony between man and beast soon crumbled and vanished.

Yet with all the materialism inevitably associated with trade and commerce, it is impossible to imagine a Champlain coming up this very river uninspired by what he saw, untouched by noble exultation over the discovery of a land unknown and never seen before. What thoughts and feelings filled him when for the first time he penetrated into these virgin forests that sucked from this river their life and their luxuriant growth? Where upon these lichen-covered rocks was then engraved the mark of highest water level in the spring? If he was a sensitive and thoughtful man, surely he must have passed through this land of pure and unspoiled beauty, forgetful of the mundane intentions of his coming, transported by its primitive enchantment!

Three hundred years later, men lacking vision to match their high ambitions broke into this wilderness and felled every last tree of the virgin forest. In the course of a few years all was demolished, all but the river which carried the logs upon its broad back downstream to the mills and thus, incongruously, contributed to the desecration of the land. And as a consequence of its own deed and betrayal—now the trees were gone and their roots were dead—it shrunk deep down between the cliffs, a mere illusion of its former turbulent magnificence. There are few reminders left of the virgin forest's crowning glories, nothing but a forgotten log of imposing dimensions caving in upon itself, a huge stub still defiant and as yet too tough and gummy to surrender to decay. Never was there any sense or prudence or even justification in wholesale planless plunder.

After the ax had done its work, fires caused by lightning and man's carelessness took easier advantage of the defenseless land. The present natural succession of mixed second growth that replaces the virgin forest, in its turn about to reach maturity, often shows the blighting scars of fire. Through the incendiary lacerations bacteria gain entrance into the hearts of the scarred trees and one by one, ere they reach their full prime, they fall before the wind.

Thus man and fire did their best to devastate the achievement of the ages. But the regenerative power of the seed and the land are indestructible.

On the west and south shores of Pimisi Bay lies the nucleus portion of our territory. The Trans-Canada Highway, carried across the south end of the lake on a high causeway, cuts through the land and divides it into two sections.

Green Woods, a lofty hall of aspens and birches, covers some eight or ten acres to Little Creek. Peak Hill occupies its western part and rises to a pinnacle above the tops of the trees. To the east on the slope toward Little Bay a dense climax stand of evergreens replaces the deciduous trees, and along the lake a thicket of aspens, willows, and alders essays a foothold all the way to the mouth of the creek. Reaching spearheads of reeds and cattails out into the shallows of the lake, a marshy meadow abruptly halts the advance of the trees and discourages any further encroachments upon the water's rightful margins. Beyond the creek rises the steep rounded contour of Brulé Hill, so named from the spectacular conflagration that took place the first night we came to live at Pimisi Bay. Fanned by a strong south wind, the forest fire leapt up the south side of the hill, making huge torches of the pines, which sent showers of live sparks over our roof. But our home was not cast for destruction that night. As the fire reached the top of the hill and began creeping down the north side it miraculously lost its momentum and died.

North of the highway, from an escarpment back of our territory, the land forms a terraced southeasterly slope down to the lake. This land is largely drumlins and morraine. Wild arrays of rocks and boulders lie wedged tightly into each other and buried deep in the ground, others are thrown helter-skelter over the top of it. The glaciers and melting waters of the past dug a series of ravines through this section, whose sides and bottoms are made up of silt and clay, some of it compressed into a shaly stratum too hard even for the roots of the trees to penetrate.

Deep under the South Ravine a confluence of underground streams creates a nest of springs which sends to the surface through silt and gravel an overflow of wonderful cool water at the rate of several gallons a minute. This constant flow of water saturates the ground on its way to the lake. A luxuriant growth of trees, denser and greener than anywhere else, follows the little stream and rises through the rich understory of highbush cranberry, hazel, and honeysuckles of various kinds. And again under their protective spread an assortment of baby evergreens are coming to life, seeded from the scattered parent trees by the wind, the law of gravity, and the red squirrels. But farther northward, around our house and beyond it, these fast-growing youngsters are rapidly crowding out their erstwhile protectors. And here a succession of new coniferous plant life is entirely changing the character of the forest floor and bird-beast habitats.

Summer in these parts reaches a climax of lush riotous growth that hides the ground under wild sarsaparilla, bush honeysuckle, seas of waist-high bracken and strings entanglements of bindweed, raspberry canes, and red osiers wherever enough breathing space is left for these humbler weeds. Through the sun-hot days and moon-silvered nights of August, summer figuratively rests from its magnificent labors until autumn announces its readiness to take over by a few dabs here and there of its vivid paint brush. Reluctantly summer gives up its heart's creations and the master artist goes to work, turning the oaks and the maples into glowing hues of blood red and the birches and the poplars into luminous gold. Ever capricious in mood and behavior, autumn often plays tricks upon the landscape, withdrawing into a masquerade of belated summer that confuses the coming-out party of the pussy willows and forces an odd strawberry bloom to open its delicate face toward the hazy October sun. But the evergreens, not to be duped by these irregular frivolities, gravely shake their crowns and branches and liberate showers of discarded brown needles that soon in a thick carpet cover the ground at their feet, until the trees stand forth blue-green to await the inevitable. In a whirl of snow winter enthrones itself upon the land, burying autumn amid its faded glories and tying up the wavelets of the lake under sheets of groaning ice. And then, when all signs of life are at last sup-

[25]

pressed under its immaculate cover, even this hard taskmaster finds time to sit back, as it were, to enjoy its own show of frost-sparkling glamour until a returning sun relentlessly dissolves all winter's efforts in tears and releases spring.

In the course of time we have come to know every tree and bush, every sapling that slowly loses its perfect miniature form as it boldly stretches itself toward the sky and the light, every windfall and rotting log that embodies a tale of its own from the past, every rock and boulder covered with mosses and lichens. We are familiar with the favored spots where the bunchberries grow, whose starry white blossoms turn into the brilliantly red berries that are the black bear's favorite dessert, with the places where the polygalas spring from their long perennial roots in mauve bouquets, where the wild columbines graciously nod their fire-red heads in places of rock and sunshine, where the prince's pines adorn the shaded ground beneath the evergreens. We have discovered where the shy orchids are secreted away in sylvan solitude, needing no companions to enhance their allure, where groups of pallid Indian pipes are likely to spring from under the leaves of wild ginseng and aster.

From the first we decided that our imprints were to mar the surroundings as lightly as possible. We cut no trails but, like the deer and the snowshoe hare, wore our paths over the rocks, around the trees and bushes. We left the thickets to grow in their own way and the undergrowth to remain dense and tangled to protect the nesting places of the birds and the hide-outs of the smaller beasts. Our house grew out of the rock, log joined to log taken from the forest, a piece of plain and humble architecture without pretensions except large room for growth and improvements. Stained deep brown like the earth and the dead leaves, with the light-shaded chinking between the logs looking like strips of sunshine playing on the walls, the house successfully affirms its affinity with the wilderness setting.

CHAPTER THREE

The Lovely

"I just saw a robin at the spring," Len announced as he came in with two pails of sparkling water. Tiny drops trickled down the outside of the pails and dripped on the floor. He filled the little tank by the door with the day's supply.

At first his words did not register with me because I was busy with breakfast. He took off his mitts and rubbed his hands. His eyes glistened in the dim light of our small kitchen.

"Louise," he went on, "spring's here!"

But still I did not catch on to his exciting message. Only a few days ago the house was sitting in snow to the eaves, and with the cold frosty nights spring seemed very far away.

Our first winter at Pimisi Bay had been hard. It had been full of trials and errors and all kinds of unknown conditions. The snowfall had been heavy and the problem of keeping the traffic lanes open out to the road and up to the spring turned out to be a major task demanding a great deal of energy. The snow had been banked high on each side of the paths, in places level with our shoulders. We had tried just trampling the snow down, but with the first thaw we discovered the disadvantages of this method. It made of the paths hard rounded ridges that were fine to walk on in cold weather when the snow gripped. But when the weather was mild these ridges became so slippery as to defy progress even with snowshoes. This was the lazy man's way and soon the snow shovels and we became great friends.

A fire in the fireplace is a wonderfully pleasant and cosy thing and a wood fire is fine to cook on. But during the coldest part of the long northern winter to keep the house warm, only moderately warm, with wood as fuel, wood fetched directly from the forest, is quite another matter. Before winter started, inexperienced as we were, we had no qualms whatever about the heating question. The forest was full of trees. All there was to do was to chop the tree down, cut up the trunk with the crosscut saw, and carry or drag the pieces down to the house in deep snow. During the coldest weeks to get enough wood to keep us warm took the whole day. Len became as hard as nails and as lean as the trees he cut down.

Then there was the difference between dry and green wood. All our wood was green. We had never thought of that. The green wood had to be coaxed to burn, but once aflame it lasted longer than dry wood though it gave less heat. It also gummed up the stove pipes and the chimneys. When the black tarlike substance accumulated too thickly, it oozed from the joints of the pipes and dripped on the floor, smelled acrid and strong, and would not wash off, had to be scraped away. Once it caught fire and the chimney belched forth thick black smoke. We stood watching with our hearts in our throats. But the chimney withstood the heat of that fire.

We had a heater-type cookstove with a large round fire box down to the floor which held a lot more wood than an ordinary range. We counted on it to do more heating than cooking, which also it did. But it was no miracle burner. Of course it

warmed only so long as the wood lasted, no more than two or three hours when stacked full in the evening. As the fire died down the frost bit into the roof and the logs and the wood contracted with loud reports. But it hardly disturbed us; we never slept more soundly than under the warm blankets in our freezing house.

Outside in the night the temperature stood at below zero. An icily cold full moon lavished its silvered reflections upon the snow, the stars sparkled. The night was eerie. Three deer came out of the shadows and meandered slowly down the southeastern slope, plowing narrow tracks like ribands behind them. The shadows cast by the trees absorbed them, then again released them to the moonlight. There was no sound, not even the crunch of the snow as the deer carefully lifted and set down their dainty cloven hoofs in the soft white stuff. Nothing—except the frost cracking in the trees with the effect of a sudden minor explosion.

Today had dawned mild. During the past week there had indeed been a feeling in the air of an impending change. The snow had shrunk, bare patches were showing, and with the wind blowing from the south the forest smelled different. As the snow melted, seeds, leaves, and other debris of the forest, accumulated and buried during the winter, came to light and now rode on top of the shrinking snow mass. In odd places a collection of light footprints suggested a bird's opportune looting of this well-preserved residue.

"A robin at the spring, did you say? Are you sure? Let's go and see it, do you think it's still there? Come on!" I was outside in the clear fresh air.

It smelled of thaw, warm sunshine, and humidity. We ran up the path toward the spring. The dead leaves were soft and wet underfoot, the snow in the remaining patches was coarse as gravel and glided away as we stepped on it. The chickadees were singing, one higher, two lower notes, bell-clear. We got to the spring and looked for the robin. We looked at each other disappointed; it must have gone. No, there it was, just a bit farther up past the spring on a branch, resplendent, its breast appearing never so rust-red as today when seen for the first time, the first robin in the obscurity of the tall trees.

The bird scanned us questioningly with its left eye. It uttered a soft note, *que-wit-wit.* Did it mean who are they? It flapped its wings softly against its flanks. It flew farther in amongst the trees, sat for a while, then flew out of sight down on a spot of bare ground. We could hear the very light rustle of the leaves as the bird turned them over in search of food. Beautiful bird! Beautiful springtime!

I turned and danced down the path in front of Len, two hops on each foot. My heart was light and gay with a wonderful

feeling of release, the sun, the air, the lovely reawakening world. "Spring's here, spring's here!" I chanted.

"There's a song sparrow down by the lake," Len volunteered, to make me feel still happier.

I was overwhelmed by all these signs of spring crowding in upon us all at once. "Where, where? What does it sound like? I've never heard a song sparrow."

"Listen!" We stopped. "I love the song of the song sparrow," Len said, "it's my favorite bird. When I was a child . . ."

Faintly, because the song came through the trees from a distance, but distinctly, first the introductory notes, then the warble dropped upon the air liquid and clear. Cautiously we approached a little closer. There the bird was, in its modest brown

plumage, the dark breast spot, the streaks, the buff-colored edges of the feathers on wings and tail, drawn sharply in the bright light of the sun. It sat on a small twig above the slushy ice with its head tilted backward, and the short bill, pointing skyward, opened and closed, opened and closed. The tail hung down slack and trembled with the effort of the bird's vocal performance.

"When I was a child . . ." Len's words struck an echo from my own past of long ago. Birds and the things of nature had the same meaning to him as to me. This was a new and wonderful realization. So far we had neither had time nor opportunity really to test our individaal reactions to the new life. But these things are inborn. His favorite bird was the song sparrow, mine had been the crested tit.

Suddenly a glimmer of better understanding came to me about the real meaning of this land that we had striven to possess for the realization of a dream rather than an end. It was real and this was the main point. The things in it were real. The situations in it developed accurately according to a logical design. The stars that penetrated the darkness of space were real, not just a distant glitter. The shimmering snow sparkle was real, not tinsel. The bird was real, not an imitation or a falsehood. The winter's hard labor we had just experienced was performed for a real purpose, not just for gain, and it had a salubrious effect upon our bodies and our minds. It had to do with life, real life; it had to do with survival.

Nature is a deep reality and whether we understand it or not it is true and elemental. Here in our own wilderness with its essence of actuality we had a marvelous chance to probe into the meanings of this saner kind of life with its purer values.

The way I started to walk when I was very young but had abandoned, the threads lost by the death of my father, I could now pick up again under circumstances and in an environment which at least in their most essential parts bore a likeness to the old life at Svensksund. And from this day I began to look and to listen in a new way. I began to see and to hear things I had never seen or heard before, because I became gradually more sensitive to everything that existed and lived beside us.

To learn how to identify a bird by its general outline, markings, and behavior as a species belonging to a certain family or order was a new and thrilling occupation, and so it remains, I think, forever new, forever thrilling throughout life with every watcher of birds.

I began to make interesting discoveries. For instance, until a brown-headed chickadee arrived upon the scene and by its brownish tints and raspy voice proclaimed itself as obviously distinct from the common black-capped chickadee, I did not know there were two kinds of this engaging little bird. The confusions I worked through learning to tell the thrushes apart before I realized the meaning of a rust-red tail, or a reddish head, or a cream-colored eye-ring, or a gray cheek, or the absence of all four, were stumbling blocks not the less real because recognition is now automatic and I can laugh at my early difficulties.

Having reached this stage, I began to take notes, naively written as if I were speaking to the birds directly—you did this, you did that, sort of thing. This seemed to lead us, the birds and me, into a more intimate relationship. It also led me into an entirely anthropomorphic appreciation of the birds and their behavior. But for a long time I remained blissfully ignorant of even the existence of that long word and certainly of its meaning and of the impediments it posed to the art of objective observation.

The great horned owl was one of the first birds to appear on my written pages. The magnificent secretive bird made a strong impression upon me; it was the wilderness incarnate and it was much more common in those days than it is today.

"Going up the river in the canoe," I wrote, "on this beautiful late summer day of August, we saw you again. In broad daylight you sat in full view in the very top of a distorted gray chicot.[1] Gravely you turned upon us your facial disk. The rusty brown coloring margined by black of each cheek and the fringe of fluffy white feathers around your hooked beak appeared very distinctly and beautifully drawn as you sat against a backdrop of shaded rock and evergreens. At deliberate intervals gray membranes worked across your yellow orbs, shutting their light off and on as you observed our stealthy approach to get a closer look at you. There was, we thought, immense dignity and aloofness in your pose and in your slow motions, as if you alone belonged to this wild and enchanting scenery—and we did not. Presently your softly feathered wings lifted and spread, hooked talons disengaged themselves from the perch, and as a speckled shadow, borne on a breath of wind, you vanished among the trees."

[1] French term for a dead tree stub.

During the years that followed this impressive encounter, the owl showed itself again many times. Once, after a series of unearthly screams and hiccups had called me out in the gathering dusk to identify the originator, I came face to face with the large bird sitting on a low branch in a tree beyond the spring, blinking and smacking its bill. Undoubtedly, a pair nested somewhere along the river between Talon Lake and Pimisi Bay for many years, but we never found the nest. Then evidences of the owl's presence became scarcer, dwindled to a few occasions when in the morning we found a small collection of furry tails under one of the feeders, all that remained of an engaging crowd of flying squirrels after the owl's nightly visit. Then nothing more. The wide-eyed flying squirrels were relieved from one of their most deadly enemies, at least temporarily.

One day in May sunny climes seemed magically to enter the Pimisi Bay area with an exotic-looking bird we had never seen before. At that time all my ornithological research was conducted with the help of Chester A. Reed's modest but within its limits excellent *Bird Guide.* Frantically, lest it vanish, I searched for an explanation of the extraordinary apparition. There I found it, orange and black matching the warm deep yellow color of the bird in the cherry tree, beautifully offset by the shining black head, neck, wings, and tail. It could not be anything else, the bird sampling our suet was, of all things, a Baltimore oriole, an amazing sight, for in my ignorance of the local avifauna I had not expected to see so colorful a bird so far north.

The next day the female, lovely in her softly demure greenish-yellow coloring, introduced herself. A few minutes later she engaged in a fight with a hairy woodpecker over dominion of the feeding tray. Soon after I came upon the male battling a red squirrel in the top of a pine.

Nothing of this registered in my mind as other than detached events without any particular meaning. My discovery of the orioles' nest hanging beautifully bulbous from a branch in one of the twin birches on the southeastern slope did not even suggest to me at that time any significant connection between the birds' occupation of the land and their pugnacity. Quite another observation, actually more sophisticated than this first instance of territorial defense I had witnessed but not understood, carried the probing of my curiosity a step further. The following year I was pretty sure the same pair returned to our forest to nest again. Both birds behaved as if they were quite familiar with the premises. But now the male's loud whistled song was much more varied and elaborate than it had been the year before. I listened with delight to the lovely notes and wondered about the reason for this. Did the bird's innate ability to sing gradually develop in skill from year to year? Or was his more elaborate phrasing acquired through imitation? The question was unanswerable, but of course the important thing was the question itself.

Later I learned that Baltimore orioles are by no means uncommon in this region, and they are also to be found much farther north. But their preference is for open parklands and gardens where the broad-leaved trees predominate. Just by chance, then, one pair, possibly in the first year of their adulthood, found within our closed-in mixed forest a limited area on the southeastern slope that answered to their requirements. And so there they nested and to this place they returned to nest again another year.

The deeper I became involved in my preoccupation with birds and nature, the more irksome I found my ignorance of the most elementary things about them. For my own satisfaction I needed some kind of purpose to which my curiosity and interest could be geared.

This was particularly important just at this time, because Len had enlisted at the start of the war and I was alone. For how long nobody knew; I was prepared to be without him for months certainly, probably for years. It was therefore necessary to fill my days with pursuits that were absorbing and worthwhile and, from that viewpoint, this was the chance of a lifetime to concentrate on the serious study of the life around me.

The actual turning-point came unexpectedly when a friend presented me with P. A. Taverner's book, *Birds of Canada.* I sat down and read it from cover to cover.

Mr. Taverner was curator of birds at the National Museum of Canada and knew his subject. But this was not what prompted me to write to him. What impressed me was Mr. Taverner's talent of turning what could have been a dry annotated list of birds, a description of species by species, what they look like, what they do, what they eat into a tale of astonishing fascination and vividness. And this I told him.

The effect of that letter was beyond all expectations. The author's acknowledgment came as complete surprise. It was richly colored with the enthusiasm and insightful humility which I later learned so characterized his gentle spirit. From this first contact a friendship developed between us, I do not recall exactly how, that turned out to be of great significance to me in my new role of serious nature student, and endured until Mr. Taverner's death six years later.

We never met and personal acquaintance did not seem necessary. By letter we discussed many things from past and present events to politics and philosophy, war and peace, always with birds and natural history as the central theme from which the digressions emanated and expanded. This was my first real contact with somebody who represented the scientific attitude, somebody with the larger vision. The way he challenged my ways of thinking without ever seeming to do so, the spur of canny encouragement he applied to urge me on, the fine realism with which he expressed his ideas always elicited my immediate and eager response. To be linked to such a giver as the fortunate recipient of gifts was a wonderful experience. Rather miraculously I had acquired a companion and a co-observer who could see the things I saw and *explain them*, even though he was not there in the flesh.

One spring day I identified a mysterious bird, so like a thrush, that sang loudly and almost without interruption back in the forest. It was an ovenbird and a flock of them had arrived from the south that morning. Their loud seesawing notes, in force and expression mounting toward the end of the song, came from several parts of Green Woods, from the southeastern slope, from the thickets around the spring and in the ravines, from the escarpment farther back. One ovenbird answered another, a third one chimed in, the voices of a fourth and a fifth blended with each other.

On this particular spring morning the ovenbirds appeared to have descended from the skies for no other purpose than to burst into song. And so perhaps they had. And having sung, they moved on "surface-hopping" from one place to the other, along the shore, inland, always northward. In those early days the ovenbirds were numerous in these parts. Throughout the breeding season their voices were heard from at least as many micro-locations as they occupied on this day of their first arrival from the south. Their boldly striped breasts, their cute strutting walk, their broad-legged singing pose assuring the maintenance of needed equilibrium during the forceful delivery of their out-pourings, all this was continually in evidence from the day they arrived to their departure and made this waterthrush one of the most familiar summer residents of our forest.

All that summer I listened to the loveliest flight-songs without being able to discover their author. I heard them most often at dusk, more seldom in the daytime, sometimes at night, and in the hours just before dawn they seemed to be performed with particular ardor and élan. Often the mysterious bird startled me by beginning its performance from somewhere close, bursting forth with those loud spaced introductory notes announcing that the main aria was about to begin. And then came the song proper, delivered as if each warbled note were fetched with tremendous effort from the singer's innermost reaches, poured from the heart, until the bird fell from the skies as if exhausted. In vain I searched for the singer returned to earth without ever spotting the trace of even an escaping shadow.

One day in July, in the role of a father with a young one in tow, one of the ovenbirds appeared at the feeding station. In the sun the feathers on his back acquired a lovely greenish sheen and the orange stripe along the crown reflected the sunbeam. By contrast, the coloring of the fledging was all dullness and suffusion with a countershaded effect that blended beautifully with the milieu, designed to safeguard the survival of the young one through the period of its immaturity. The father was silent and intensely preoccupied with picking from the ground tiny specks of suet dropped by the other birds. High-stepping out front, he led the two-bird procession across the dappled shadows. Ever so often he turned in his tracks to pop a morsel of food into the mouth, hastily agape, of his begging child.

A few days later the ovenbird came walking past my door, this time alone. I stood on the threshold watching him. The next instant he disappeared. At the same moment the sharp introductory notes of the flight-song came to me from right overhead, followed by the remarkable warbled sequence. At the end of this performance my astonished eyes perceived the ovenbird the very second he touched ground, almost in the identical spot whence he had vanished. Thereupon he stepped out of sight as if entirely innocent of ever having left the earth or uttered a note. And the riddle of the flight-song was solved at last.

This was a year of many new discoveries and one thrilling event followed upon the other in my world of nature. My capacity for observation improved markedly. New sounds impinged upon my ears with greater intensity and selectivity. I began to detect movement and form belonging to the creatures of the forest where in earlier days I would have heard or seen nothing. A new bird, correctly identified, added itself to the last one on my list. And so it went.

However, with the loss of novelty I found myself inclined to lose interest in the new bird. I concentrated all my attention on looking for the next unknown bird that might be lurking in the bushy entanglements, just waiting for me to record it. This is the great danger of "listing." It is a pitfall quite common to the novice bird-watcher. One is greedy for the sensational at the expense of experience in depth. One forgets that the less spectacular is often the more significant detail of birdlore, which provides the knowledge that makes the expert out of the watcher. But in spite of these beginner's failings that afflicted me, each new experience added, almost unnoticed and not without lasting gain, its golden coin to my collection.

On the last day of May I heard a soft clicking, *tuck—tuck-tucktuck—tuck*, uneven in rhythm, a sound I had never heard before. As I crossed over to Green Woods whence it came, the sun was getting low and its beams seeped through the trees, making the smooth white bark of the birches shine golden. Dusk coming on and these strange notes from a strange bird gave me a feeling of mystery and subdued excitement.

I caught sight of the bird almost at once. I pursued it as it flew into a tree, stumbled over rocks and undergrowth with eyes glued to the slim form, hoping not to scare it away before I had time to note all its markings. The bird was as large as a blue jay, brownish-gray in color with a faint wash of green on the back, white underneath. Its long flirting tail was as straight and wide as an ordinary footrule, and marked every inch or so on the underside with a penciled bar in black and white. It had a finely curved bill, all black.

The sight, especially the form of the bill, pulled forth a memory from long ago. I knew this kind of bird, I had seen it before, although I remembered something of a darker color and barred markings, a cuckoo. Could this be a cuckoo? Cuckoos in North America? But there was at the moment no time to check with the books.

From somewhere else in the distance came the same clucking notes, sharper and louder as a second bird approached. There it was, another cuckoolike bird, perhaps the mate of the first one. With soft languid movements it advanced toward the first bird, remarkable movements I thought they were, whose meaning I could not rightly assess. At that moment the first bird flew out as if to meet the second one, but halfway across the distance that separated them it changed direction abruptly and flew off, giving very soft *tuck-tuck* notes. Come on, come on—was this the meaning this plausible maneuver suggested? The next instant the two birds came together on a horizontal branch, the briefest airiest meeting of their light, faintly greenish bodies, then they separated, flew apart, vanished among the trees. I stood entranced looking at the spot where they had just been. Color, form, setting—simplicity, harmony, beauty!

The books said that two species of cuckoos may be found in these latitudes of Pimisi Bay and that the black-billed is the more common of the two.

Summer passed, and autumn, filled with arduous birding. The first snow came and at dawn one day in early December my ear once again caught an unfamiliar note, this time a whistle. Dimly in the dusk of the morning I glimpsed a grosbeaklike bird vanishing among the trees. It was too dark to go after it and the sighting of the ghost slipped my mind until, in broad daylight, my eyes fastened upon an incredible sight.

The broom I held in my hand clattered to the floor. Scarcely more than ten feet away out there on the ground was a brilliant red bird, its head adorned with an elegant pointed crest. A velvety jet-black area around the large pink bill, extending to the twinkling dark-brown eyes and forming a bib under the chin, was the only divergence from the bird's overall scarlet plumage. There was no need to consult the books on this one. I had looked at its picture many times, envying those who might count it among their common birds, never dreaming that so exotic an apparition would ever sit in the midst of the snow of this northern landscape.

The next day, to my surprise and delight the cardinal was still there. From then on, every new day with this red bird in our inhospitable white world was a gift of grace. Could it possibly survive the rigors of our northern climate? On days when the temperature sank to below zero the cardinal emerged from its roost in a small dense spruce with a patch of frozen breath stuck to its back where its head had been buried among the feathers of the shoulder. It sat on its feet to keep warm and nibbled nuts with the other birds, but otherwise it showed no sign of being uncomfortable or affected by the cold. When at Christmas time I had the house gaily decorated with red wreaths in the windows and the red bird was perched on the peak of the roof or sprawled bathing in the deep snow, one motif in red matched the other.

On a mild day in late February the cardinal sang for the first time. In the top of a tall pine he sat framed in green with his breast aflame in a beam of sunshine and his full throat bubbled with these new mellow whistled notes; and the harsh northern environment put its own stamp of distinction upon their delicious clarity and modulations. Every day for a month and a half the cardinal sang, and I was the only one who heard him and listened to his song. At the end of this time he was still alone without a partner of his own kind. One day he vanished and for a while the sun went out and the silence lay stark and oppressive over these woods where the cardinal had been but was no more.

Naturally I shared the whole history of the cardinal's stay at Pimisi Bay with Mr. Taverner. He was particularly interested because that winter saw an unprecedented invasion of cardinals eastward and northward. My bird had come some two hundred miles farther north than the main body of this incursion. After this, reports of cardinals being seen or visting feeding stations began to come in more frequently from this part of Ontario, even from as far north as Kirkland Lake, two hundred and fifty miles north of Pimisi Bay.

Sixteen years later a cardinal once again appeared at Pimisi Bay. This was a lone female arriving from the north on a dark November evening. She stayed three days and then vanished. Several years later, in late June, another male cardinal, singing as he passed through our area northward, provided a rare summer record. But, so far as I know, no nestings have been reported, and thus the presence of the cardinal in our latitudes must still be considered only accidental.

The war went on and on interminably. Len went overseas with his regiment and the prospect of our reunion and his happy homecoming appeared inordinately remote.

With every new discovery my desire increased to turn my bird-watching into something more meaningful. Real bird-watching—when you sit and watch every move and detail in the behavior and the activities of certain birds known person- ally and then record all you see and hear—was beyond my ken. It did not even occur to me. Finally I turned to my friend and asked, "What can I do?" Certainly the opportunity was mine, all I needed was a purpose, a channeling of current activities in-to a definite direction.

Mr. Taverner's answer came back promptly: "Why not take up bird-banding?" He also told me where and how to apply for a license. He proposed himself as one of the two sponsors who are required to vouch for the applicant's ability to identify birds. The other was Hugh Halliday, the well-known writer and bird photographer, with whom I had recently come in contact by correspondence. With these two names on my application form, I was soon in business as a full-fledged bird-bander. My relationship with the birds changed dramatically. Personal recognition became a thrilling possibility. The bird was no longer just a member of a certain species but a special individual of unique character, whose life history could be followed from stage to stage.

As banding activities go, I can claim no spectacular achievements of any kind. One or two foreign birds, banded elsewhere, and less than a dozen of my own birds recovered abroad out of a total of slightly more than twenty-five thousand birds banded are on record in my files. This adds very little to our general knowledge about, for instance, their migration, their mortality and ages. But for my own close-range study of bird behavior, into which my bird-watching finally led me, banding proved to be a significant accessory. This is, indeed, one of the most profitable ends of bird-banding.

Three of the most interesting recoveries of my own birds ought to be mentioned here. One of these was a young pigeon hawk hatched in a tall pine on the slope of Brulé Hill. We rescued it from starvation after its parents had disappeared and raised it to adulthood on beef liver and dog food. Early in September the young hawk migrated, and the next summer it was killed at Deer River, Stasca County, Minnesota, in the same latitude as its birthplace but about a thousand miles farther west.

Few house wrens come to nest in our forest. The environment is not particularly to their taste. They favor fairly open places where a cavity of some kind is available. One year, nevertheless, an unmated male wren arrived and established his territory around the house with a birdbox in the cherry tree as the main attraction. Being alone, he filled the place with his singing from morning until night, full loud lovely songs. Even from a distance a passing female could not have missed hearing him. But no prospective mate appeared to put the feminine touch to any of his many cocknests, constructed in every conceivable niche. In early July he departed as unmated as he had arrived, and in September four years later the sweet bird was killed against a power line at Walker, West Virginia, about seven hundred fifty miles due south of Pimisi Bay.

Most of the blue jays of this region are permanent residents, provided they can find enough food to see them through the winter. Early one January I banded one of them, a bird of the year as shown by its plumage which lacked the black barring on certain wing feathers. It stayed around the feeding station all that winter and in the spring nested not far away. At Christmas time, almost a year later, it was shot at Henderson, Tennessee. Thus, in the fall of its second year, this blue jay migrated in a slightly south-southwesterly direction and was caught by death about a thousand miles from its birthplace.

A year before Len finally returned home safely after five long years, two naturalists and bird-watchers, Doris and Murray Speirs, found their way to Pimisi Bay.

Perhaps it was symbolic that on this particular day the rose-breasted grosbeak should greet them with a full-voiced concert of mellifluous notes; that the ruby-throated hummingbird, first for the season, should have chosen just this day for its return; that a flock of pine siskins, hitherto unknown to me, should flit about in the top of a tall tree so that I could learn to recognize their raspy twitter. This was the first time I came in personal contact with people with whom I could share exciting experiences, who knew how to look at birds and nature with the discerning and objective eye. And in the years of fruitful association and friendship that followed I learned from them the best and proper ways to study birds. I learned how to appreciate the richness of my untouched forest and to draw therefrom the knowledge and understanding that would eventually surpass my earlier highly unsophisticated efforts.

Through them I was to be introduced into a new intellectual environment which culminated in my first meeting with Margaret Nice. World famous as a student of bird behavior, this remarkable and gifted friend took hold of my purpose, and my work, and the whole of my thought life in fact, and as gently as the wind blowing from the south in the spring, as gently and as surely, changed all of it.

Two

CHAPTER FOUR

An Exercise in Tolerance

I shot the red squirrel. It fell dead. A thin stream of its life's blood soaked into the ground beneath the inert form. I stared at it.

A little while ago the squirrel had tried in vain to jump to a half coconut filled with sunflower seeds. The coconut, intended strictly for the birds, was suspended from a string stretched between two trees, out of reach, I thought, of even the most enterprising squirrel. But this one was in possession of a high degree of persistency, and the frustration of not being able to achieve its goal put a resourceful twist to its endeavors. The squirrel ran up one of the trees and bit off the string. Down crashed the coconut. The squirrel squinted at the wealth of seeds spilled on the ground, ran down, and gorged itself upon the loot. This developed into a routine maneuver that never failed. And suddenly my patience ran out.

At that moment I took no account of my own frustration which turned into a fit of annoyance reinforced by a need for vengeance. Several things justified these feelings. First, I was interested in birds and not in squirrels and therefore the birds must be protected against the trespassing and food-stealing squirrels. Moreover, the squirrels' reputation was bad. Stealing the birds' food was only one of their minor sins. Had I not with my own eyes seen a red squirrel sitting bolt upright on a stump twirling the head of a tiny junco nestling between its frontpaws as if it were a nut, to the accompaniment of the junco parents' loud distress calls? And another time I heard a scream followed by ominous silence. When I got to the spot I found a pair of veeries attacking a red squirrel with a fury rarely displayed by these gentle thrushes. Why? Because the sight of the squirrel feasting upon the exposed red liver of their fledgling aroused their vehement protest, naturally. They dived at the predator, tried to unseat it, chase it, but never got close enough even to touch it. The squirrel only jumped around so that it always faced the attacking birds and continued to enjoy its ill-gotten meal.

These episodes, and also the idea acquired in childhood that the squirrels were "bad" characters, turned me against them and indeed against any other creature that was likely to interfere with those from which I reserved all my sympathy, the birds. Up to this moment I had fought the squirrels—futilely, for their desire to eat was irrepressible; unreasonably, because I never made clear to myself either their real position or mine.

What is good and what is bad? I know the answer now: all and nothing. Everything called bad may on occasion turn into a blessing and likewise all that is good can under certain circumstances become an unmitigated evil.

Suddenly the iniquity of my deed struck me full force. The squirrel was without fault, an innocent. Naturally the thwarted urge to eat moved it to do just what it did, an act of distinct survival value no matter how the animal arrived at doing it. Persistency and the energy that fires it are among life's most significant ingredients. Their suppression often destroys success.

And everybody, even a red squirrel, is entitled to his own measure of success. The red squirrel had merely followed a true and logical tendency and for this reason alone was worthy of my whole-hearted approval instead of extinction.

Disturbing thoughts! Stupidity and injustice are uncomfortable terms when applied to one's own mistakes. Prejudice is a dreadful hindrance in any endeavor to acquire realistic understanding. But this was the goal I had set myself long ago. The inept idea of dividing nature into parts—these are the good ones and those are the bad ones, some to be overly indulged and others disliked, disdained, persecuted—was a greatly confusing stumbling block.

Naturally the realization of all this did not come overnight, but the incident was a turning point. Many relapses impeded progress. But at least I understood now that the inclination to kill was wrong. Drastically and thoughtlessly I had played with the life and death of creatures that lived around us and had no means of defense except their utter innocence. But to dissipate the confusions of which I was guilty required a deeper penetration into the problems of predators and prey, of life and death, devoid of sentimentality. A prolonged effort was needed to learn about the lives and the requirements and the reactions of these "bad" characters, the red squirrels in particular. And in the account of my endeavors along these lines I shall use Kicki, an irresistible female squirrel, as the prototype who will represent all the red squirrels I have ever known. She was in fact the Red Queen of another Wonderland, who metaphorically took me by the hand and introduced me to many phases of the red squirrels' remarkable and intimate world.

How the rapprochement between Kicki and me started I cannot remember. It was probably just one of those things that happen, based on the subtle attraction that develops occasionally between two characters whose reactions to each other are more favorable than otherwise. For my part I wanted to be friends with Kicki in order to learn at first hand what it was like to be a red squirrel. That I stooped to employ artificial aids in attaining this objective may be forgiven on the premise that the goal justified the means in mutual measure. My lard pudding, a concoction of rolled oats, fat, and water, was and is a delicacy universally approved by all the animals of our forest from the black bears to the chipping sparrows. A small chunk of it, named a courtesy ball, wrecked many a barrier of fear and distrust erected between man and beast since the days of the lost Paradise.

As for Kicki, the beginnings were too casual to suggest any feelings for or against. She took me in her stride as she would the next tree on her arboreal highways. But because dash and boldness were features infused from birth into her character, she left herself open to such insinuating things as courtesy balls and me.

Being a typical representative of the red squirrel tribe, Kicki differs from the common throng only in that each of her distinctive traits is etched with reinforced emphasis. There are no two ways about anything she does. The situation that stimulates her into action makes her perform exactly according to the true need of the moment. Although moods and external circumstances often influence her responses and lend to them a variety of nuances, the results are by and large never out of line, depending of course on the standpoint from which they are judged.

Kicki's whole life and being is dominated by nervous tension that expresses itself particularly well in the movements of her bushy tail and in her vocal contributions. Her large eyes, that seem never to blink and whose prominence is somewhat enhanced by a ring of small light-colored hairs, give the impression of a slightly overactive thyroid. Yet with all her amazing vitality she is an expert at snatching catnaps at the most unlikely moments. She just stops and naps, then and there, for a few seconds or a minute or two, ample allowance, apparently, for restoking her energy. Only in the privacy of her snug nests and hideouts does she give herself up to sleep with the same consummate abandon with which she pursues action during her waking hours.

Her days are filled to the brim with important business that carries her through the year with zest. After she finishes rearing her young during spring and summer, she begins hoarding for the winter. After this is completed, she goes on to build or to refurbish her winter nest, a bulky affair tucked into a bushy conifer that stands in a sheltered place. She constructs the nest for the most part of dead leaves tied together with strips of cedar bark. During the winter she keeps alive on her hoarded goods, supplemented by buds of spruce and fir and whatever the feeding station has to offer. Finally, after some ado, she accepts a father for her prospective young and goes to work preparing the nest for the happy event. At this juncture she loses all interest in dalliance and arbitrarily dissolves the ties with the father, at least temporarily.

I have the greatest respect and admiration for Kicki as a mother. She usually houses her babies in an abandoned nesthole or a knothole in the trees high up away from terrestrial dangers. Latterly she moved into a new apartment under the eaves of the porch, in the space formed by the overhang of the roof and the boards enclosing the ends of the rafters. Through a narrow aperture between the wall and the boards she squeezes in and out. She lines the nest with dead grasses, straws, strips of cedar bark, bits of tissue paper, and hairs from her molted winter coat, to make a snug bed for each new litter. To facilitate transportation she manipulates the stuff with her dexterous front paws into tight balls which she carries home in her mouth.

By early May motherhood imprints itself upon her whole being. She looks disheveled and worn from the strain of nursing. Often there is an expression upon her face—or so I fancy—as if the blessings of motherhood were not quite what they are made out to be and hence should be compensated by a more generous distribution of courtesy balls. Anyhow this is the way she acts, although naturally the nourishment the babies drain from her requires replacement by measure. Later on, as the period of weaning begins, she quickly recuperates.

All through this time Kicki remains strictly and efficiently vigilant. She allows neither outsiders nor babies any liberties. Once during play one of her kits took an awful tumble through the slit entrance of the eaves nest down into the rose-bush and then scampered off to hide among the lilies, none the worse but scared to death. Upon hearing its whimpers of dire loneliness, Kicki rushed to its aid. Instantly locating the youngster, she grasped it by the scruff of the neck and carried the now perfectly limp and silent burden up on the telephone wire beside the eaves. Precariously balancing herself and the baby on this trembling support, she proceeded to squeeze and push, push and squeeze the child through the narrow cranny to safety, an awkward and acrobatic feat few mothers could have performed.

In due time she literally shakes off motherhood with the same perfect sense of timing as she entered upon it. Under her nose, so to speak, now appear fruits, berries, and other growth in such profusion that all cannot be eaten at once. When wealth of one kind or another overwhelms her, a strong inclination always directs her to tuck away into any convenient shelf or cranny what she cannot make use of at once. Thus, driven by this urge to pluck the lot, she begins hoarding.

Though it is still only late summer and ample time is left before the first snowfall, she is suddenly possessed by frantic haste. Toadstools begin wandering through the undergrowth, seemingly on their own, with Kicki hidden under their top hats, laboriously propelling them. She races up the trunks of the evergreens and nips off the cones, one by one. She races down, picks up the fallen cones, and runs off with them, tips first. If she carried them in any other way, she would never get them through the narrow corridor to her selected cache. With her face a sticky mess of gum, she works from dawn to nightfall, allowing herself scarcely enough recess to feed and to rest.

Just how strong the urgency to hoard is in a squirrel, Kicki ably demonstrated one year when because of a drought nothing except clusters of small brown cedar cones hung on the trees and the toadstool harvest failed. First she stripped all the cones off the cedars. Then, when she could not find anything else to hoard, she collected small rocks. In ardent pursuit of her seasonal task she ran with the stones in her mouth, every so often dropping them because they were heavy and awkward to carry. She picked them up again and then carried them, jumpety-hop, over rocks and other obstacles, through the tall bracken, to her storeroom, with the same enthusiasm as if they were cones. In the winter she gave no inkling of being put out by her "bread" having turned to stone. Judging by the alley of tracks her feet wore in the snow from the feeding station to the cache under the balsam fir, it may be presumed that she felt no pinch at all and as usual rode the crest of the wave in her own indomitable style.

Kicki arranged her caches in a variety of places, under tree roots, under rocks, in unused holes dug by other animals. Once she took possession of our cellar, to which she gained entrance through an unscreened ventilator. The stores she amassed here defy either count or description. Presumably, the proportion of the space she found at her disposal under our floors induced her to go far beyond her usual limits and needs, with respect both to the volume and to the time she allotted to her harvesting. On another occasion she dropped a large supply of spruce cones into the shallow never-freezing water of the spring's overflow. In February she dug a tunnel through the snow to this cache and presently came up with one fresh cone after the other. In a strip of sunshine at the base of a tall poplar she sat down, picked off all the scales, and devoured the seeds with relish.

[57]

Sometimes, as I watched her, instead of running off with her load to her storeroom she hastily buried it at random. With quick paws she dug a little hole, put the stuff down, patted it into place, then covered it at arm's length. Apparently these extracurricular burials stemmed from her strong reluctance to go directly to the cache while she was being watched. In fact she merely disposed of her load quickly and conveniently; in effect her performance distracted my attention and kept the location of her head office secret and safe. But she never revealed whether she came back for the buried store or merely forgot all about it.

Kicki possesses a keen sense of ownership of the space surrounding her nursery, her winter chambers, her caches, and other special places. She claims these spaces simply by being there and supports her title to them in various ways. There she lives, although more than once I have met her quite far beyond the more or less staked out limits of her domains. On the ground as well as in the trees she established habitual roads and avenues for her own convenience. Habit is for her—as well as for me—a great boon to existence. Indeed, some of these trails of hers on terra firma actually come to appear worn from the repeated passage of her pattering feet.

In defense of her territory Kicki treats trespassing members of her own species most harshly. In fact, especially during the periods of her annual cycle when her possessive urges reach a peak, she hardly tolerates another red squirrel on the premises. These peaks generally coincide with times of greatest activity that are also times of greatest stress—for instance, when she is nursing her young, at the height of the hoarding season, and in winter when food is scarce and keeping alive is a major business. This aggressiveness is natural and it is a true tendency. The rejection of interference when the demands of self-preservation need to be met is not antisocial behavior but fully justified. On these occasions the individual triumphs over the group, and in the end it is the individual that maintains the species.

The incitement to hostilities works on Kicki by degrees and is brought to a culmination by means of a set sequence of actions. There is no question of deviation from this pattern of behavior; only the speed with which the climax is produced depends on the situation and the particular way that the intruder's approach plays upon her responses at the given moment. Four main stages of stereotyped actions bring her into a fighting mood: pseudo-mastication, loud chatter, drumming with the hind legs and, finally, explosive chatter.

By studying the variations in speed and intensity with which these actions are performed, one can easily tell exactly how the squirrel feels and what is going to happen next. The mastication is a chewing motion with nothing in the mouth, pure pretense, similar to the way old people sometimes chew when they get excited and cannot control their chins. Birds, and other animals, too, resort to the same trick at a time when their ire is aroused but their response as yet fails to be crystallized into decisive action because the situation kindles too complex a range of reactions.

With the loud chatter Kicki proclaims that she is getting bolder. "I'm master here, get out," the expression on her face seems to say. Impatiently she drums her hind legs. Hares and rabbits also drum with their hind legs loudly and suddenly, and so startling is this sound that the pursuing enemy is often stopped in his tracks for an instant, the precious instant that gives the pursued a breathless chance of escape. The hare is frightened out of its wits and the next second flees like the wind, zigzagging wildly to throw the enemy off scent, off balance, anything to gain a foot of distance between them. Kicki's drumming, by contrast, contains more pugnacity than the hare's and indicates that she is getting really angry and means it. She emphasizes the threat by bursting into explosive chatter, a kind of staccato rapid-fire performance uttered with such passion that she actually shakes from emotion and her tail twitches eloquently.

In all these preliminaries an intimate interaction develops between her own and the opponent's reactions, a process within each that alternatingly oscillates between urges of prudence and audacity. This wards off actual combat and directs their next moves. At this point the whole affair usually dissolves, with Kicki discreetly being left in undisputed control of her domain. But, if not, like a dwarf demon on the rampage, Kicki flings hesitation to the winds and dashes at her adversary. Spiraling up and down the tree trunks after her foe, leaping cross-country in high style, she finally throws herself bodily at the interloper. The impact upsets the other and the two roll together as one ball of fur, hissing, spitting, clawing, biting.

Sometimes when Kicki happens to be surprised at close quarters while having dinner at the squirrel plate, she reacts full throttle. Her tail twitches violently, she screams. This scares and enrages the rival. As the latter moves to counter her challenge, Kicki rises upon her hind legs to her full height, looking like a miniature bear ready for the devastating embrace. In rhythmic hops she advances and the usual melee results, with moves faster than the eye can follow, leaving in the end a few drops of red blood spattered over the battle scene.

Her relations with other animals Kicki handles with consummate plasticity. At such encounters experience influences her approach and so do the size and the temper of the intruder.

I do not know which one, Kicki or the beautiful white ermine as it enters the squirrel's domain, ought to be judged the most fierce. Lithe and inimitably graceful, the weasel in winter dress with its eyes shining like beads and the black-tipped tail bringing the elongated white body to an elegant end emerges from a snow tunnel dug by the squirrel. It dashes quickly hither and yon in a seemingly haphazard search for titbits, finds one, dashes back out of sight. Out it comes again, tugs at a piece of chicken carcass too big for the tunnel entrance, pulls it aside, stops, listens, looks—intent, utterly alert, its triangular face raised on a strong muscular neck overemphasized in size as compared with the slenderness of the rest of its body. Now Kicki catches sight of it. Both dash into the same tunnel—and I sit tense waiting for the signs of the bloody drama that surely is taking place inside. But the next instant the squirrel shoots out of the tunnel, all in one piece, and the weasel peeps forth and observes the scenery with a perfectly innocent look on its face. Suddenly, the two tear at each other again. They fight in the

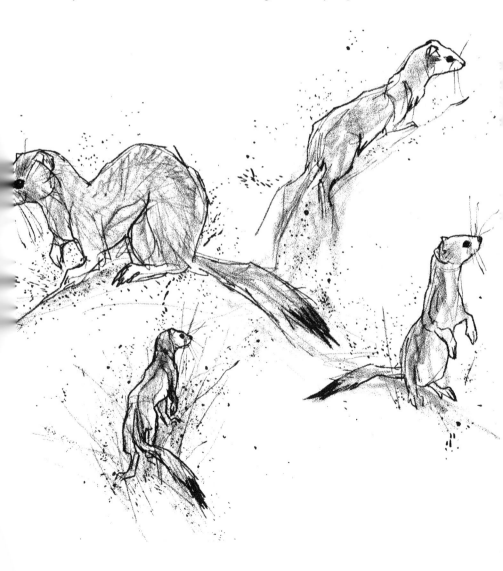

opening of the tunnels, like cats, never touching each other, but with sparks of temper and fury flying, a seesawing battle, each alternatively attacking with reckless daring and withdrawing bristling, ears flattened, teeth gleaming. They are so evenly matched that nothing whatever comes of the encounter and it dissolves harmlessly.

The only leporine inhabitant of our forest is the snowshoe hare. It is almost one and a half times as large as the red squirrel. In the spring Old Doe leaves the swamp where she usually winters and takes up residence in the neighborhood of our house. There she and her families, one or two, sometimes three, a year, stay around until late fall. Some years there are more of them, in other years many fewer hares go back to the swamps for the winter. This fluctuation in the hare population usually repeats itself every ten years or so. The ones we have known personally have as a rule survived about four or five years.

Since we got grass to grow on the rocks around the house Old Doe has been very happy. In the early morning when the dew is on the green grass she loves to sit with all four feet gathered under her and eat her fill. Faithful to the habit of most of the forest's denizens, she rests during the forenoon. About the middle of the afternoon she emerges to spend the best part of her day abroad, eating, hopping around, sometimes engaging in various social activities when the demands of her progeny in the hollow under the great log leave her some free time. In the night she takes another period of rest. In the lives of all animals, this wonderfully appropriate division of the twenty-four hours into rhythmic alternations between action and quiescence, if left undisturbed, effectively contributes to their well-being and keeps them in top condition.

Old Doe is also very fond of bread and rolled oats—and so is Kicki. This therefore is the medium that quite frequently brings these two together. When Kicki finds Old Doe enthroned upon one of her favorite feeding spots she first essays intimidation and races madly to and fro in front of the hare's twitching

nose. This startles and confuses Old Doe. With all four feet off the ground at the same time she leaps away from the source of irritation, leaving the field open to Kicki who loses not a second in supplanting her on the disputed site. There she sits chattering away, making lightning turns always to face the hare just in case Old Doe might sneak an attack upon her. But even a hare's timidity has its limits. Quite often Old Doe elects to stand her ground and she imparts this decision by snapping at Kicki. In the face of such odds the red fury can do little else than beat a strategic retreat, though never without her usual bounce.

One might expect that the deer's intrusion upon Kicki's premises would set her back on her heels. But nothing of the sort happens. For the most part Kicki ignores the deer and the deer take scant notice of the small fry of the forest. This is the safest, and there is really sufficient room for them all. Their food requirements, their modes of living are different and thus create no conflict of interests. Yet the crossing of their paths at the feeding station brings them within the critical distance of each other. With unparalleled nerve Kicki begins to run in figure eights in and out between the legs of the towering ruminants, an ingratiating maneuver, an incongruous and anomalous invitation to play on Kicki's part, plainly exposing the mixture of feelings that possesses her, fright, daring, appeasement. Konrad Lorenz, the famous student of animal behavior, gives an account of a small puppy's behaving in exactly the same way at its first meeting with a very large black dog.[1]

Startled at first, the deer become slightly skittish. But Kicki is too nimble to fall foul of their hoofs. As all animal-watchers well know, the abnormally large provocation is apt to elicit the anticlimactic reaction. Just this is what happens to Kicki. She stops, sits up in front of the deer. Holding her stomach tight with her front paws, she tests the air with her sensitive nose. With prettily cocked ears Goliath looks down upon David. For

[1] Konrad Lorenz, *Man Meets Dog* (London: Methuen & Company, Ltd., 1954).

a long instant, both of them trembling lightly with arrested excitement, the two touch noses. The secret communication satisfies. The deer resumes browsing and the squirrel runs off.

Mute communications of this kind exchanged at unscheduled meetings between the most unlikely participants are not at all uncommon. With her pouches full Shortytail, the chipmunk, runs in great haste on the way to her hideout. Suddenly she comes face to face with the flicker which is picking ants on the slope in front of the house. Startled by the unexpected and close encounter—the chipmunk almost ran into the flicker—both freeze motionless. Then, a little gingerly but without hurry or hostility, the chipmunk's nose meets the bill of the flicker. That is enough. Without further ado each resumes his, her, previous occupation.

These episodes are good examples of nature's manifold ways

of avoiding wasteful conflict. It is of special interest that the absence of disturbing factors, which are apt to increase nervous tension and often bring about distorted and exaggerated responses, quite commonly favors the adjustments necessary for peaceful contact between animals in the wild, whose relations may not under all circumstances be quite so benevolent.

Kicki's associations with birds are a matter of some delicacy and quite different from her rapport with other animals. Generally speaking, the red squirrel is a vegetarian whose favorite foods include nuts, seeds, mushrooms, fruits, and berries. Comparatively rarely, because the season is limited, the squirrel eats the eggs and the young of birds; under certain circumstances involving intense nervous tension, it may attack and kill adult birds.

In the first case, the number of nests that the squirrel misses during a season is quite astonishing. This, of course, also depends on circumstances and may vary greatly in different localities. Part of the reason for this is the squirrel's inclination to keep to its own most traveled trails. Nests situated off these routes enjoy a certain immunity. But when the squirrel finds a nest, nothing stops it from picking it clean, one by one, of eggs or young. The squirrel's persistency, even against great odds, is legendary. On occasion the little animal's fine nose detects the edible contents behind the wall of the gourdlike cavity belonging to a hole-nesting bird. Should the parent bird bar the entrance and in this strategically safe position use its bill in effective defense, the frustrated squirrel attacks the wall itself and attempts to break an entry. Only the solidness of the wood coupled with the sustained vigilance of the parent birds safeguards from the squirrel's wildly tearing teeth whatever lies at the bottom of the nest cavity.

I have never known an instance of true predation by a squirrel upon an adult bird, but a squirrel may attack a bird under special provocation or in abnormal situations. The banding cages, if not closely watched, may on rare occasions prove a deathtrap for a luckless bird caught with a squirrel near or actually in the trap with the bird. Sudden loss of freedom causes a bird to panic. Fright sometimes kills outright. Fright expressed by wild movements—a bird's beating wings and its reckless efforts to get out—is contagious. This throws the squirrel entirely out of character and, unless the panic stops as the hapless bird quickly finds an opening for escape, in the twinkling of an eye the squirrel is a killer. The skunk's, the weasel's, the raccoon's traditional ravages in the farmer's chicken house may often enough be the result of similar tension-producing situations, when the animal's natural snooping predacity traps it inside with a mob of dangerously panic-stricken birds. The word for the madness that affects the killers is therefore neither ferocity nor voracity, but fright.

Otherwise Kicki harbors no malevolence toward the birds, though her innate aggressiveness leads her always to insist on dominating the scene. She allows no frivolities and she acts accordingly whenever the situation demands it, by making short runs or sudden jumps at the birds to keep them in line. Only the crows and the blue jays occasionally turn the tables on the squirrel. They, and the barred owl, are the only birds I know that can outwit a red squirrel. All of them use the same technique: persistent pursuit accompanied by wing-flapping. The last is the essential part of the ritual that usually assures the pursuer's success. Its effect upon the squirrel is confusion at first, but this rapidly changes to fright and then to panic, and with that complete disarmament. With respect to the crows and the blue jays, the issue is never more serious than the squirrel's loss of a courtesy ball or a piece of suet, which the birds espy as it is being carried away and covet. But when the owl is on the scene, the life of the squirrel is in the balance. By a series of maneuvers that often seem awkward and aimless, the owl works the squirrel into a state of abject distraction by driving it into

places, out on branches, into corners, where it must backtrack or take inordinate risks. Sooner or later the inevitable happens. This is one game that the red squirrel rarely or never wins.

What exactly caused our neighborhood animals suddenly to indulge in exaggerated and often destructive behavior was for a long time a puzzling problem. That frustration played a large part was not difficult to divine. An unusually successful breeding season, bringing about a serious temporary overcrowding of squirrels and other small animals, as a natural consequence gave rise to overly intense competition. The effect of these circumstances did not come to light until an interesting state of affairs developed quite by chance, resulting from changes I made in the set-up of the feeding station.

By this time the elimination, either by shooting or displacement, of any animal whose behavior interfered with our purposes in some way had long since been rejected. Displacement, which at first seemed a humane substitution for the gun, was abandoned after two of the displaced animals, a red squirrel and a young woodchuck, gave indications that this was not true. The red squirrel returned within a week, but the young woodchuck, which had started homeward upon release and kept oriented in the right direction for over an hour, did not make it. Obviously neither animal tolerated the displacement. The gamut of unknown and frightening dangers these little beasts had to run in entirely strange surroundings is not difficult to imagine. Familiarity with its environment, the knowledge of where the good hiding places are in an emergency, may spell the difference between life and death. And previous experience with neighbors and other occupants of the land must give an animal, if not a sense of security, at least a far better chance of escaping dangers than an altogether unknown place can provide. Hence displacement is a hardly less drastic measure to impose upon an animal than sudden death.

Other measures, therefore, had to be devised to counteract

the obviously rising tensions and I tried rearrangements at the feeding station. To start with I separated the feeding places. I figured that if each animal could be persuaded to find its food in a certain place without having to endure too much interference from the others, a great deal of frustration might be avoided. So the bird-feeders were made squirrelproof by means of shields, upside-down funnels. The squirrels got their daily rations served on special easily accessible plates. Old Doe was persuaded to look for bread and grain on certain rocks—that is, until the squirrels and chipmunks got wind of this, although despite clashes complaisant sharing between them and the hare was not unusual. Finally, the raccoons and the skunks got their own dishes too. Fortunately they did not all feed at the same time of the day.

Everything worked well until competition reached what seemed to be a critical level. Being the most highly strung of the lot, the squirrels showed the effects of the situation most seriously. Among them were five whose reactions were remarkably different from one another.

Squirrel 1 was by nature an aggressive female of Kicki's type. The squirrelproof feeder affronted her. With unrelenting tenacity, day by day, she concentrated her efforts upon its conquest, running up the post and into the funnel. In her frustration at never getting any farther she compensated by establishing her own special territory around the post and opposing the approach of everyone, her own kind in particular, with exaggerated fury. Erect upon her hind legs she would advance upon the intruder in jerky hops and with front paws held like those of a boxer about to deal the knock-out blow, she would fling herself at him, screaming at the top of her voice. With each thwarted attempt to scale the feeder, the quicker and more violent were her attacks. She went completely crazy, mercilessly attacked Old Doe as she passed by in all innocence, clawed at our feet, snarling, whenever we came within a certain distance of the feeder—certainly a most interesting example how irritation beyond endurance can sometimes explode into exaggerated and irrelevant behavior.

The squirrelproof feeder also jarred the nerves of Squirrel 2. But, unlike the first, this one did not try to conquer it. Instead the little animal relieved its frustration by digging holes in the ground below the feeder, small neat holes, dozens of them, at distances of a few inches to two feet from the feeder post. It is well known that animals, including man, under stress often perform acts quite unrelated to the situation at hand, and the so-called "sparking-over" activity is an important ingredient in the process of dissipating the effects of stress.

Squirrel 3 found her way into the house by chance one day when the door was open. There she discovered the place where I kept the courtesy balls, and from then on she slipped in whenever the door was ajar. Later, when she found the door closed, she adroitly learned to push in one of the window screens, Thereupon she loped around the table, picked up a ball, perched on the back of a chair, and proceeded to feast upon it. The remarkable deliberation with which she performed all these actions set her behavior in sharp contrast with that of the other four squirrels, and her easy adaptability thus furnished her with an outlet whereby she avoided frustration.

Squirrel 4 was much more highly strung and as a result she reacted with greater intensity. Instead of approaching me with confidence to receive her courtesy ball as she had done up to then, she stretched out full length along the ground, her hind legs spread-eagled behind her, her tail with its tip quivering curved tightly over her back and head. In this highly exaggerated pose she crawled to my hand. When I was not there to serve her, she attacked the house. Frantically she gnawed at the window frame, at the sill, at the door. She made a dreadful mess of all three. Whenever possible I tried to forestall her by offering her the prize she was after. But—and this is the most interesting part of the story—if the door was open and she could easily have slipped in to get what she wanted, she seemed entirely unaware of the opportunity. She gnawed at the open door with the same frenzy as when she found it closed. The passion with which she performed this activity nevertheless gradually dispelled her built-up nervous tension.

When I first knew her, squirrel 5 was certainly not vicious by nature. But she reacted to the stress-filled situation and the strong competition in a way that made her vicious in act. Earlier, when she had mistaken the tip of my finger for a courtesy ball, which happened at times, she had merely closed her teeth on it gently and released it. Now she snapped, and as stress increased she snapped more viciously, drawing blood. Under pressure her behavior degenerated still further. She began to molest the birds and whenever she succeeded in cornering one she was apt to kill it. It became a habit, a true case of the blooded tooth and nail. She caught one downy woodpecker in one of the banding traps, killed it, and then ran away as if she had nipped off a cone and let it drop. She went for another woodpecker, but that time I saw her and stopped the murder. She was a sorely stress-ridden creature but not a killer in the true sense.

The whole situation got more and more out of hand. Hot mustard and a strong solution of mothballs painted on the woodwork of the window and the door partially discouraged the destructiveness of squirrel 4; closing all the traps and eliminating other places where the birds could get caught by the chasing squirrel staved off the killer tendencies of no. 5. But neither preventive was foolproof.

Then, finally, almost imperceptibly, things began to change. What happened? Only this: autumn changed into winter. The animals that could not find sufficient food from the forest and the feeding station drifted away, others vanished for unknown reasons, leaving conditions in a state of greater stability and balance, where life still caused stress but in other ways and to a somewhat lesser degree.

Nervous tension that builds up under stress seems to be one

of the most vital instruments in nature's self-regulatory systems. It tends to direct the living creature into channels of behavior that in the strangest ways counteract upsetting pressures created in the course of existence and thus ultimately subserve the restoration of harmonious balance.

I never knew the exact time of Kicki's disappearance. In some way it was eclipsed by the presence of another squirrel, one just as alert and aggressive as she was, one pervaded with the same amount of nervous energy as she always possessed, one who, according to law and order, filled the empty space so that there was no loss.

CHAPTER FIVE

Sprites of the Northern Forest

Dawn is the matchless hour. The break of every new day invests this hour with a distilled purity and effervescence. The light, returning once again, filters roseate through the forest and inundates the wilderness. It slowly unveils each separate outline of slope, rock, and tree. Softly it touches all of them with its transparent loveliness until at length the transformation from night to day reveals the last secrets of darkness and is complete.

The snow lies soft and muffles all sound. The wind is asleep, I do not know where, perhaps in the tops of the pines or at the foot of the cliff, tucked deep into the crevasses. The silence is so full and so strong, so alive, that my ears ring with it, with the subtle vibrations of the land, the snow, and the sky arched above it. Of a sudden the wood of a tree cracks loudly with a sharp metallic detonation from the hard frost. But the next instant the silence, rendered more hushed then before, settles over the land once again.

The sun loiters at the horizon. With a shaft of soft light it illuminates the sky, announcing its intention to rise soon. There is still no sound from any living thing. But the imminence of awakening makes the silence implausible.

A moment later, far away, the song of a bird drops its harmony into the sea of silence. The song is a simple ditty composed of three whistled notes, one high and two lower ones. In a fractionally different key another song of the same kind answers. Both are repeated together with the effect of a two-toned stroke of the violin. Soon a third voice gives echo through the snow-lacy woods, and still another, each one coming from a different direction.

This is the chickadees' hour of song. In the deep frost and the glittering snows of the early January days the wind of change touches them. Their urge for musical self-expression awakens. Their singing is the ordained prelude to the annual inauguration of their reproductive cycle, which in birds that do not migrate comes early and proceeds very slowly. And their dawn song is the best.

The chickadees sing sitting upright on a twig and addressing their oratory to the world at large. Their song is an utterance of careless freedom, of independence, of self-assertion. It presages their growing disinclination to wander about in small flocks and their new tendency to divide into pairs. But this is a slow process and subject to much ritual. The outward and inward changes that produce these new impulses are dependent on a variety of mutual interactions between the chickadees and the environment, which effect necessary encouragement while at the same time exercising due restraint.

Presently small flocks of chickadees emerge from every place where the evergreens stand thick and sheltering. A wisp of snow floats off into the air as one of them touches a tuft of pine needles and releases a minor avalanche. Other chickadees appear among the trees and branches, two, six, ten, eleven—I count them all. Instantly the still air and the motionless trees are

touched by sparkle and animation. Grace, frolic, elfin passion, and inexhaustible zest enter upon the scene with the black-capped chickadee. And in the east a flushed sun peeps over the horizon, sending a dazzling beam over the hills and the tree tops to set them afire.

The chickadees look like fluffballs with beads of frost clinging to their whiskers and to the peripheral tips of their erected plumage. Small cakes of ice stick to the backs of some of them where their breaths froze during the night as they slept with their heads tucked into the feathers of the shoulder. Others appear with their tails twisted and bent sideways. These chickadees roosted one to a cavity and in the cramped space filled with the humid warmth of the tiny body their rear adornments temporarily set into those informal shapes. But there are only a few of these, because cavities are rarely available for chickadee roosting. Nuthatches, creepers, woodpeckers, all lay claim to them. Hence most of the chickadees sleep outside on the evergreen twigs, entrusting themselves to their stored caloric energy. Their built-in heating mechanism raises all their body feathers to form an insulating aura around them, which keeps them shivering but tenaciously alive throughout the long chilling hours of the northern night.

On bitterly cold mornings when the thermometer has dipped to twenty or thirty below zero, the chickadee requires some time to limber up. Tucking first one cold foot well up into the down on its belly, and then the other after the first one warms up a bit, the bird nibbles at a piece of food to make a start. But the deep-freeze is numbing. On the southeastern slope down by the lake the chickadee seeks out a spot facing east where the hill gives shelter from the north wind. There the double source of heat created by the reflected radiance of the sun upon the snow assists the warming of the tiny body.

The chickadee peers into the sun, shivers, sinks down upon its feet again as if to fill itself with yet another dose of warmth and light. It yawns, then shakes itself. And saturated for the moment with the solar contribution, it flies off with all its feathers sleeked along its flanks, undaunted, to meet the claims that life imposes on the living.

On stubby wings the chickadee dashes, swoops upon its aerial way from tree to tree, taking a route mapped out beforehand by habit and the memory of food once found upon this very circuit. It stops, clings to a spot, and from a myopic distance examines folds and crevices in the bark, around the twigs and branches, searching for the minute morsel it always finds in spite of all repeated foraging. In winter, secrecy is no requirement of the chickadees; to proclaim by cheeps and twitter whatever happens close at hand—the finding of a piece of food, objection to a rival, or any threatening sign of potential danger—is then their leading policy and reciprocally of service to them all.

Sooner or later all the chickadees' routes lead to the feeding station. Sooner or later, provided they come close enough to be guided by eye or ear, the chickadees traveling from north to south or vice versa find their way there. In winter the peak influx usually occurs in January, but competing peaks sometimes develop also in November and March. Older birds, coming from a distance to spend the winter here, arrive early in the fall and leave late in the spring, because to them the route is familiar and they travel direct.

The chickadee's life is short—one, two, rarely three years. But a few live longer. One of mine, a female with a yellow band on her left leg, disappeared at the ripe old age of nine years. Several other nine-year-olds are on record, but that seems to be the greatest age to which a chickadee can aspire.

In the beginning the feeding station was to me just a nice place to which the birds of the forest could be attracted to please the eye. But soon the fascination of watching superseded all other pleasures derived from it. The rare bird and the strange animal still continued to provide their moments of special thrills, but what the ordinary bird did proved to be far more exciting and challenging. Why do the chickadees lift their head feathers as if tipping their tiny black hats? Why do they puff up all their body feathers? Why do they stiffen and spread their wings? Obviously, all this has some special meaning, an underlying reason that has to do with communication and social behavior. Why do they "point" their bills upward—there is no better way to describe the gesture—as they confront one of their fellows? Why do they gape without either eating or uttering a sound? Why do they chew with nothing in their bill when they are excited? What is the meaning of this and of all their notes and calls, their imperious *chicka-dee-dee-dee*? These and other questions crowded in upon me. And I wanted to be able to "read" these moves and attitudes and learn something about how a chickadee felt and the motivations behind these acts. So I began to watch in a different way and, naturally, the more I watched, the more I saw. A realization of the immense importance of the finest detail of each movement in relation to the prevailing situation began to dawn upon me. Very gradually I learned to read the signs and to decode the mysteries and it is quite amazing how far into the essential things of life this watching leads the watcher.

Half a dozen chickadees arrive almost simultaneously and perch on a wire near a feeder. The line-up is the result of their simultaneous desire to eat. But they stop at the wire and each one raises its bill into the air and points it toward the neighbor on the right, then repeats the same act to the neighbor on the left. This continues for well-nigh a minute with the birds "bill-pointing" alternately to the left and to the right. The performance is amusing to watch; it looks as if the birds were greeting one another repeatedly with distant politeness.

But nothing is further from the truth. The simple set-up is in fact quite an involved story. To "point" the bill at a fellow chickadee expresses a threat with much the same meaning as we would put into pointing a finger at somebody in anger or fright or with a desire to keep him from doing something. Indeed, similar feelings also prompt the bird. Now the chickadee's bill is only a few millimeters in length and all black. But look at a chickadee's head and note that the jet-black cap and bib and the pure white cheeks form four triangles whose apexes converge upon the small conelike bill. This remarkable design makes the chickadee's whole head appear as one large beak. Think of this next time you look at a chickadee and see if it is not true. This is what other chickadees see when an opponent points its bill at them: "Beware! Keep your distance! Don't overstep on my territory!" I was astounded when I first discovered the illusion and I soon learned that other watchers had seen it before me. Spots, stripes, patches of color, intricate and contrasting designs, the stimulating illusions occupy a prominent place in nature's chest of tools.

I also found that an area, aptly called "individual distance," exists around each bird, within which the intrusion of others is not willingly tolerated. This space protects the privacy of the individual. It is portable. It varies in size in different species and sometimes at different times in the same species. For instance,

Konrad Lorenz tells us that for starlings this area is as large as the reach of their bills. For the chickadees on the wire the area was larger than the reach of their bills; it was a circle of about four or five inches in diameter.

Here then is the full story of the performance on the wire. Six chickadees experience at the same time the same impulse —that of going to the feeder. Their almost simultaneous movement to get there inhibits their approach to the goal and they all stop on the conveniently suspended wire. There they come to sit slightly too close to one another. So they begin "pointing" their bills at one another to prevent the neighbors on either side from encroaching upon their respective individual distances. For a poised minute the emotions of all six are in perfect balance, allowing the birds neither to flee nor to fight nor to advance upon the feeder. But then a piece of peanut butter drops from the feeder to the ground, a most opportune event. Two of the chickadees, their urge to eat irresistibly aroused, dive on the morsel; this breaks the spell with lightning suddenness and the "pointing" parade dissolves. The two on the ground separate, one moving on to the feeder and the other fly-

ing off with the lion's share of peanut butter, while the rest, having lost interest, disperse, their volatile attention focused on other engagements.

To have a wild bird come to my hand of its own free will seemed to me for a long time an utterly remote possibility. It is different, I argued, in the populated areas where the animals become conditioned to the proximity of man and corrupted to a certain extent, led astray from their wild ways. Here in the great natural wilderness animals and birds of another caliber are conceived, uninhibited, mercurially free. But I did not reckon with the power of the seed.

Peet was the first chickadee that introduced itself to me as a unique individual. He sat on a twig and rather in fun, expecting nothing, I offered him a sunflower seed. To my immense surprise he alighted on my hand, looked me in the eye, and curled his feet around my finger with flattering confidence.

I had no intention of taming him. Taming is to coerce an animal into a constrained unnatural intimacy. It would have destroyed all Peet's spontaneity, all the freedom of our relationship. But from the moment Peet came to associate me with the seed, the bond was forged between us. And it was irreversible.

This was the first time I introduced the sunflower seed to the chickadees. I am positive that Peet was seeing this kind of seed for the first time in his life, although it may have looked like something else he had seen. No other feeding stations existed in the section of the wilderness where Peet first saw the light of day. Yet not only did he recognize the seed as food, but he knew precisely what to do with it. His manner of holding it fast with both feet, opening the shell with a series of smart taps, and then with a deft twist of the bill extracting the kernel, was innate.

After that Peet's arrival in gaily bouncing flight from the top of the tall pine directly down on target, never missing the tip of my finger, or his insouciant entry through the open window to look for a seed that I had hidden behind the cream jug just to see how quickly he could find it, were sources of never-palling delight. The realization that from Peet's viewpoint I personally played a highly insignificant role and that the object of his fearless interest was nothing but the seed did not in the least lessen my enthrallment.

Peet got his name from the soft note he always uttered as he approached me. To say that this was his way of attracting my attention is near to the truth, because this was exactly what it did. But that was not its true meaning. In chickadee parlance the *peet* note means: "I'm dimly aware of danger!" Thus, in fact, in spite of his boldness and his pioneering in a chickadee's relations with man, he never approached me entirely fearlessly. His innate cautiousness was still present in so large a measure that in spite of previous experience he was at all times perfectly ready to escape. I could never lay my hand on him, even touch him ever so lightly. To cross his individual distance was impossible. But he could alight on my nose and pick a seed from my lips with utmost assurance. His own initiative made that situation quite different.

In the course of the years other Peets replaced the first one at various intervals. One of them always sang as it approached me, *chittereee-chittereee*, notes recognized among chickadees as a challenge to fight. Another one burst into a series of loud and emphatic scolding notes, *chick-dee-dee-dee*, expressing thereby an ambivalent measure of fear and aggressiveness, which was just its way of bolstering its own courage at the moment of approach. A third one never said anything but instead wafted its wings at my ear or cheek in a startling close fly-past, displaying in this way the mixture of boldness and timidity it felt when it wanted to get its seed. Even in our most intimate moments, the chickadees never lost their wildness.

Peet brought practically the whole chickadee population to my hand that first winter. By his own unpremeditated example he induced the others to overcome their timidity to the required degree. Some of them, the few possessed of the same pioneering spirit as Peet, took little inducing. Others whose nervous tension always slightly inclined toward the urge to escape never became quite sure of themselves and needed to make two or three quick intentional return-to-perch dashes before alighting on my hand. They looked searchingly into my face, then quickly picked their seed and were gone. I often wondered exactly what reassured them? Was it just the absence of an untoward movement on my part? To most of them, coming to my hand was largely a matter of what one chickadee can do and get away with, we too can do. They did, and the seed was their reward.

What was I in their eyes? I hung my coat on a branch and instantly Peet went to the coat. He examined it carefully and looked into the pockets. I was there, but he paid no attention to me until he had reassured himself that the coat hid no seed. Only then he looked at me and he came, and there was the seed.

The last time Peet came to my hand he was on his way from the feeding station to his nesting territory in the northwest ravine. He was deeply preoccupied with courting his mate. As I tentatively held out a seed to see if he would notice, he left her and came for the seed. I thought he might tender her the offering, but that was not in the program this time. He cracked the seed and ate it.

When and how Peet died I never knew. Nor did it matter. He disappeared, that was all. When separation is inevitable as it always must be sooner or later, this is a lovely way for a friend to take his leave—to be there and then just to be gone.

Blue Bird, so named because of the blue band that encircled his right leg, was a highly independent individual. Although he stubbornly rejected all invitations to come to hand, he constantly reminded me of Peet and could well have been one of his descendants. He had the same insouciant ways, the same open-mouthed aggressiveness, accentuated rather than tempered by his Lilliputian size in relation to the world in general.

In most situations Blue Bird's fighting impulses surmounted other incitements, sometimes even that of hunger, for no other reason than that he was so made. When he voiced his challenge-to-battle cry, I knew at once that somebody had fallen foul of him. The sight of my fur collar enraged him. Incongruous as the resemblance seemed to me, he obviously regarded it with the same intense hostility as he did the weasel. At any rate his reaction was the same. He flew into a state of high excitement, cheeped at the top of his voice, fluttered about, and flapped his wings, thereby attracting every other chickadee within earshot. And together they staged a mob scene around me that would have embarrassed an even less innocent furred apparition than I was. When caught in so ignominious a situation as having a trap shut upon him, Blue Bird emerged on his back, fighting mad, with my little finger firmly closed around his neck to prevent him from breaking a wing. He fixed me, the offending giant, with a pinpointed stare and pinched hard any vagrant finger within reach of his plierlike bill. And as he lay there with his claws tightly enmeshed, the legend was plainly written in the depth of his eye: "This outrage is perpetrated without my leave, I'll have you understand!"

It was quite in character that Blue Bird should be tempted to supplant Green Bird the instant he perceived the latter on the coconut feeder. To alight on a feeder when another chickadee is having its dinner is at no time a peaceful overture. Through many trials with few errors Blue Bird had learned its success. But this time Green Bird surprised him. The latter refused to take the cue from the high and mighty one and as Blue Bird alighted on the rim Green Bird held on. He sat upright with his tail spread wide and gaped. His nape feathers rose and fell in eloquent evidence of the moods that possessed him—what to do next, attack or flee?

[85]

For well on half a minute the two sat on opposite sides of the coconut and weighed back and forth in a veritable tug of war of personalities. Each bird alternately pushed forward, pointing his bill at the opponent, then withdrew gaping, indicating thereby his temporary armed retreat. When Green Bird showed no other sign of wavering, Blue Bird allowed himself to lean farther forward, gaping and pointing at the same time. In such close proximity, the combination of these two aggressive moves carried a measure of reinforced meaning and increased threat. Green Bird answered by repeating in precise detail every move Blue Bird had made. Neither of them uttered a sound. But the gaping bills acted upon their sensibilities in exactly the same way a verbal battle acts upon people. It increased nervous tension to a climax. Once more Blue Bird pressed forward, bringing his bill a fraction closer to Green Bird's nose.

This was Blue Bird's victory move. Suddenly Green Bird's position became untenable. Beating his wings in a vain attempt to maintain it, he toppled from the coconut. Alone, Blue Bird pointed his bill into the air, finding this safe outlet for his overcharged tension. Nobody noticed him, so he picked his seed and flew off.

Although Blue Bird brought this scene to a smart enough conclusion by sheer bravado, he undoubtedly had an active ally in the fact that Green Bird's hunger had quite likely been somewhat appeased before Blue Bird's arrival. Nor did Green Bird's yielding in the end mark him as a faint heart. His home grounds were in Green Woods. There he lived and nested many years, visiting the feeding station every day except during the time when he was busy raising a family. For two reasons Blue Bird could not enter these premises without being put to rout. With each yard Blue Bird found himself farther away from his own home grounds and from the feeding station where his aggressiveness earned him a high-ranking place in the chickadee hierarchy, the incentive to fight slowly declined within him. Contrariwise, Green Bird's self-assurance reached its height right in his own dooryard. This is a natural and proper ruling.

In late summer and early fall while Blue Bird was absent during his molt, Green Bird had his innings at the feeding station. He often indulged in prolonged gaping sessions with some hapless fellow who dared contest the right to a perch on a feeder on which hung no "private property" sign. The form that the end of such a session took always depended on the degree of spunk possessed by Green Bird's current opponent. These contentions sometimes involved acts in the same style as those of the man on the trapeze, when the opponent hung on to his perch swinging upside down or right side up in defiance of Green Bird's wing-flicking and toe-pecking attacks. Green Bird's favorite pose of threat included the ballooning of his contour feathers, which made him look like a toy porcupine on the ready, and thus with wing tips stiffly dropped and tail rigidly depressed and fanned he advanced upon the object of his disapproval. Sometimes when necessity dictated a further elaboration on the enlargement of his body, Green Bird would rise full height on stiffened legs and wobble like a slightly inebriated tight-rope dancer. None of the other chickadees could stand up to this awesome demonstration for any length of time.

Red-blue was banded when she was very young. It was not difficult to establish her sex, because her wing measured from the bend of the wing to the tip of the primaries was very short. She also squealed. So far as I know, male chickadees do not squeal. But when a female is or fancies herself exposed to acute danger in her nest hole or as she is caught in a trap, she utters this strident cry, which is something between the spitting of a weasel and the hiss of a snake. The owner of the predacious paw trying to probe into the chickadee's cavity soon discovers how startling and disconcerting this cry actually is.

In the spring Blue Bird emerged from several wild chasing

contests with Red-blue as his partner. Closely escorted by Blue
Bird, Red-blue now existed within a magic circle, a small defended sexual territory somewhat larger than her previous area
of individual distance. Thus the pair traveled together along
their habitual feeding routes, she leading the way from tree to
tree in bouncing flight, he following, eating little, watching
over her ever on the alert.

A certain spot along the path leading to the escarpment attracted them more than any other place. To them the most remarkable thing there was a tall poplar stub so old and rotten
that it no longer stood alone but leaned against the voluminous
branches of a vigorous red maple that stretched a foot or so
over the top of the stub. To this place the pair returned more
and more often. With every return, the more securely they
established their exclusive ownership of the land around the red
maple and the more their isolation from others of their own
kind deepened.

The task of selecting the nest site fell upon Red-blue. On the
chance of finding the likely spot she flitted gaily from stubs to
saplings to trees, found nothing to her satisfaction, and flew on,
always closely attended by Blue Bird who seemed to follow
proceedings with keen interest without getting himself involved. Red-blue looked at the dead top of a birch, a tall
spearhead crumbling with decay, where a pair of chickadees
had last year excavated a doorway over a foot long before they
finally hit upon a place solid enough to hold their cavity. She
examined a defunct birch sapling not more than four inches in
diameter where another chickadee's nest had been housed a few
years ago, a very tight fit indeed for a five-and-a-quarter-inch
bird.

Pecking a little here and giving certain spots minute scrutiny,
Red-blue pursued these activities more or less as a set ceremonial, which worked up to the final decision at exactly the
time when the mood for excavation came upon her full force. I
cannot believe that she was not aware of the leaning tower

against the red maple all this time. She circled around it, sat at the top of it looking down into its heart, she even pecked at it, so she knew the consistency of its decaying wood. What more did she need? And then one day in the early morning, as the newly arisen sun struck the top of the red maple with a reddish beam, I found her and Blue Bird engrossed in the labors of excavation, not digging a hole from the side but from the top of the stub down into its center.

Well, this was an unusual place for chiseling out a nest cavity—open to the heavens! But the question of rain need not have bothered me, for the beautiful large-toothed maple leaves took ample care of that in due time.

With the formal establishment of the territory and the nest site the behavior of the pair underwent remarkable changes. Gone was their insouciant twittering, their light-hearted conspicuousness. Now they were two birds of completely changed character, moving about with studied stealth. When I trespassed upon his property Blue Bird "froze" motionless in a spot strategically related to the nest site. His stillness belied the presence of both bird and nest. Of course I knew what he was hiding but he did not know that I knew.

I tested him by coming a step closer. He blinked an eye, and I knew then that he was intensely alive to every move I made. My approach introduced a conflict—to stand his ground or to flee. He started to chew, nervously moving his empty bill, and I knew that his tension was mounting, so I withdrew behind a bush. For a minute or two he remained sitting where he was, looking, blinking. Then, as I made no further move, he relaxed slightly. He pecked on a twig, he started to preen a wing, stretched one leg through the wing far back. Watching him, I could almost feel by sympathetic induction the relief these activities provided him. He hopped to another twig. By now he was almost convinced that I had left. I said almost, not quite, for he took ample time over every successive move he made, as if giving me every opportunity to pop forth again should I by chance still be there. He made abundantly sure he would not be taken by surprise. But once he could no longer see me, he gravitated toward the nest, prompted by an urge stronger than fright, stronger than the threat of an invisible intruder.

In Red-blue the start of their reproductive activities brought on a curious change of voice. Everything she said she now pronounced hoarsely and these raspy utterances gave her a peculiar distinctiveness she had not had before. Her behavior changed also. She relinquished the precedence she had formerly taken over Blue Bird, leading the way during their foraging trips and presiding over their nest-building affairs. She had spells of reserve and of indifference, alternating with excessive submissiveness. When this mood came upon her, she pursued Blue Bird, crouched at his feet, stretched her bill toward him and shivered her wings like a baby bird and begged to be fed. She invited him to trespass upon her personal area, to come close to her. Gradually she broke down his reluctance to give up his own precious individual distance. And as Blue Bird obliged by tendering her a morsel, excitedly for her movements stirred him, her begging demonstrations reached an ecstatic climax. One early morning when the air was limpid and honey-sweet, she crouched before him, her wings loosened from her sides and trembling, and begged—but this time not for a morsel of food. And Blue Bird responded, lightly, swiftly, with the fleeting touch of a caressing wind.

Time passed. In the early morning of Midsummer Day I paid them a visit. Their behavior had undergone another astonishing metamorphosis. Abandoned was the blinking eye, the chewing on nothing, the need to preserve the deep secrecy of the nest. All their activities were brashly out in the open—loud twitterings, excited flying about, self-exposure, nervous tension. Several times Blue Bird dove upon my head, never touching, but so swiftly and closely that I ducked involuntarily. Highly excited, Red-blue alighted on a horizontal branchlet right in front of me and no farther than two or three feet away. She teetered with her tail deeply depressed and spread like a fan, her wings dropped from her sides. She moved along the branchlet and without loosening the grip of her toes around it she tipped over and dropped head down, then swung back up. She repeated this performance again and again, like a windmill rotating down and around and up.

I gazed at her in utter fascination, and then for an instant took my eyes off her. There—there was the answer to her extraordinary exercise. On the rim of the nest entrance at the top of the leaning stub perched the fluffy figure of a very new-looking chickadee. We call demonstrations like Red-blue's "distraction displays." And whatever the actual feeling may be that motivates the performer they generally have the effect of diverting the alien eye from the precious contents of a nest. On the spur of the moment Red-blue was driven to act in this way. There was I, the intruder within her private zone. There was her vulnerable conspicuous ready-to-leave fledgling escaped from the protective enclosure of the nest, the fruit, I say, of her and Blue Bird's six weeks of toil and patient care. The excitement, the exposure, the intensity of the stimulus demanded the exaggerated and spectacular response.

To let this momentous family scene run its due natural course, I withdrew behind a bush. But the parents were not deceived. They continued to act as if under pressure of dire danger. They kept flying around the nest stub and shooed away with exaggerated impetuosity everything that moved on legs or wings. They swept up to the nest opening with loud twitterings, then dropped down and away without entering.

This maneuver excited the youngster no end. It followed the movements of the parents with intense interest. Each time the old birds approached, the young one expectantly opened its mouth to receive the habitual morsel, then cheeped loudly in disappointment as the parents flew away without obliging. This went on for some time. Finally the youngster could resist no longer the accumulating inducements. It took the leap into the wide world, a prodigious act in the life of the young bird. Blindly it relied upon its untried wings as they took it triumphantly over a distance of almost thirty feet. Hesitating where to make its first landfall, the young chickadee wobbled, missed its footing, but made it safely in the end. And there it sat fluffed and secure, viewing the surroundings with a knowing black eye.

At the nest another fluffy-head already had popped up to replace the first one. Thus one by one the children of Blue Bird and Red-blue popped up from the safety of the nest. Each one hesitated briefly while the excitement of the moment and the parents' movements did their prompting work, and then launched itself into the unknown. When the fifth one had left, the nest was empty.

This was the last time I saw Blue Bird. But Red-blue survived to the ripe age of eight years. As she grew older she developed all the traditional traits common to the Peet lineage, boldness, independence, aggressiveness. Her sex notwithstanding, she rose high in rank among the chickadees.

After Blue Bird's disappearance she took unto herself an unbanded mate. With him she vanished. Months passed before she returned to spend the winter at the feeding station. Her prolonged disappearances, which became a habit, did not detract one iota from her authority. No matter how securely another chickadee might have installed itself in her absence among the highest ranking of the flock, she always came out on top. *Veni, vidi, vici!*

CHAPTER SIX

The Nomadic Tribes

Dawn, always the dawn! Day dawns upon a fairyland forest shrouded in snow. The first snowfall of the winter came during the night. Overwhelmed by the white mass some of the slender young trees trail their tops on the ground, their trunks forming a splendid arch. The sun bursts upon this wonder world setting a million stars alight on every white surface. There could be no heaven more magnificent than this.

This was the time when they came, these nomadic tribes, the colorful finches, whose comings and goings are always irregular and unpredictable. And suddenly their twitters and songs fill our quiet white wilderness. The abundance of seeds of the evergreens, the alders, the ashes, the maples directs the movement of these birds. They come out of nowhere in the midst of winter and a single bird, or a pair giving their ringing calls, precedes the larger flocks, the scouts ahead of the coming invasion. The next thing we know they are here and they roost at night in the tall pines around our house.

And now in the early morning the air suddenly fills with exquisite music, the dawn chorus of the northern finches. Nothing is to be seen, no visible movement, just music, continuous,
warbling, *sotto voce*, anon increasingly slightly in volume and
then dying down again to the softest whisperings. Whose notes
are the sweetest? Those of the goldfinches or the crossbills or
the pine siskins? I do not know. But the birds are easy to recognize by their voices as they sit hidden among the thick
branches, uttering the characteristic themes that belong to each
species. For a long time they remain on the nightly twig singing

softly, music boxes concealed in the tops of the pines. And then . . . the music stops. The birds are gone and I did not see them go.

In this way the great invasion of northern finches began one winter twenty years ago. One of the reasons for their coming was obvious. I never saw so many cones. Beautiful long cones with drops of clear resin suspended from their tips, glittering in the sun, hung from the top branches of the white pines. Set two years before, these cones were now ready to liberate their elegant winged seeds. From a distance the white spruces looked as if tinted rust-red right down to their middles, strangely suggestive of death until one got closer and discovered that the trees were far from dying but thickly decked with small elongated cones. Along the top branches of the balsam firs crowds of oblong cones stood erect, some looking like empty spools because their scales with the seeds attached had already been shed. And in the bogs small budlike cones clung in great abundance to the branches of the black spruces and the tamaracks. A simultaneous harvest of such a variety of conifer seeds occurs only occasionally and at long intervals.

Plenty of food, plenty of birds! The conifer seeds are well suited as food for the finches, and to find the rich supply the birds move from one place to the other. Having found it they

stay. Having stopped they attract others with similar tastes. The presence of one flock suggests food to the others; their numbers increase so long as the food lasts. Conifer seeds have a high caloric value, and the bills of the finches, some stout and strong, others curved in adaptive ways, are good tools for picking the seeds from the cones, ridding them of their coverings, and mashing them to pulp. With this kind of food the finches need grit and they also have a marked liking for salt. They find this relished combination on the highways in the winter. During the great invasions this predilection proves to be a death trap to hundreds of them. The slaughter is sometimes unavoidable, for the birds have a way of sitting tight on the road and flying up only in the last split second before the vehicle bears down upon them. To entice them away from the roads we established our own salt licks. The birds found them and from these assembly points I was able to follow the unfolding story of the northern finches.

Occasionally throughout the fall I hear the clear flight notes of the crossbills, *peet-weet, peet-weet,* and sometimes I catch sight of two or three of them silhouetted against the sky, bouncing merrily in their characteristic undulating flight on their way across the lake. Toward the end of November the purple finches appear, five to twenty in each flock. They find our pile of wood ashes; they sit in the warm stuff and eat it. A few places where spilled dishwater discolors the snow also attract them. They need no further invitation. Small flocks of other finches also find our feeding place and toward Christmas time I get the first high counts of white-winged crossbills and pine siskins.

In the black-spruce bog, a place full of mystery and surprises, I find the white-winged crossbills. Even in the midst of winter the muskeg is spongy underfoot and one has to step gingerly lest the snow suddenly give way and the foot plunge into a deep hole of brown muck. The notes of the crossbills come to

me from a distance and lure me on. The sun shines and the snow is soft and deep. A crisscrossing pattern of well-trampled paths running off in all directions discloses the unseen presence of a number of snowshoe hares having their early forenoon siesta in some convenient spot. The old tote road gives better footing and I follow it through a thick underbrush of willow and red osier to a stand of towering tamaracks. And here, busy pilfering the tiny seeds from the cones that look like brown rosebuds, are the white-wings clinging to the branches of the trees amid a lively exchange of musical conversation.

After a while one of the females detaches herself from the crowd and flies across the road into the top of a black spruce promptly followed by her mate. Presently the bright rose-colored male, his black and white wings flashing in the sun, rises

perpendicularly into the air upon rapidly beating wings. A prolonged ringing trilled note accompanies this flight. With the
melody bubbling from his throat he slowly gyrates this way
and that. He looks like a splendid decoration suspended from
an invisible thread being buffeted gently to and fro by a light
current of wind. Having made no noticeable impression upon
his audience, the bird descends into the spruce top next to the
female's. Suddenly he catches sight of me standing there watching them and he utters a burry warning note. But the next moment he forgets about me, and the female in the top of the tree
once again commands all his attention. With several sweet
notes, *tweet-tweet-tweet,* he prepares us for the concert to
come. He breaks into song, continuous, prolonged, the song of
a canary but muted, slightly hoarse in delivery, composed of
deliciously warbled trills interrupted by series of *tweet-tweet-
tweets,* the tweets often held much longer than the warbled
notes and pronounced with lingering emphasis. Thus, in the
middle of the winter, an orgy of musicality inaugurates the
courtship of the white-winged crossbill.

A few days later the banding trap near the salt lick shuts
upon the pair and I have a fine opportunity to admire the details of their plumage. The basic color of the adult female is
dove-gray, darker on the back and lightly striped. The feathers
of her crown, cheeks, and flanks are tipped with golden yellow
under a light suffusion of brown, and the rump is shining yellow, the brightest of her markings. The contour feathers of the
male are a deep rose, darkest on the crown and brightest on the
rump where they are washed with yellow. Only nature, the
master painter, could design such a combination of shades in the
two sexes of the same species. The tails of both birds are satiny
black and so are their wings; two white wing bars and delicate
white edgings of some of the wing feathers greatly enhance
the birds' appearance in flight. Their curved crossed bills seen at
close quarters are a revelation of finely sculptured form.

As I put the band around the female's leg she bites and

screams, fetching the sound far down in her throat. She turns around in my opened hand, gets her legs under her, and hurriedly departs, sped on her way by the shock of affronted freedom of movement. But the male in an attitude of supreme resignation—do with me what you will—lies motionless in my hand, his dark-brown eyes following every move I make. As I tip my palm gently and he rolls off, he falls free to a point midway between my hand and the ground before quick as lightning he spreads his wings and takes flight.

Together with the white-wings, the red crossbills and the pine siskins belong to the truly nomadic finches. Except by coincidence they rarely return to the same place to nest. As the breeding season approaches, wherever food is plentiful, there the birds settle to perform their reproductive functions. The finding of food in suitable abundance may on occasion even hasten or delay breeding. This is especially true of the red crossbills, who are highly dependent on the cyclic seed-setting of certain conifers; these birds have been found nesting in every month of the year. To lay their eggs at just the right time, in a place where there is no lack of the specific food upon which their young thrive, is of paramount importance.

The lovely red crossbill and the demure little pine siskin have much in common. Both are given to dawn singing. Like the white-winged crossbill, both have exquisite flight songs incorporated in their courtship rituals, but while the male white-wing rises vertically on beating wings, the siskin and the red crossbill float from the top of a tall tree out into the air. On rapidly fluttering wings the male circles above the object of his attention, giving voice to a continuous highly melodious warbling song that lasts and lasts through circle upon circle until the bird's energy is exhausted and he dives headlong and silent into the shelter of a nearby evergreen. Both species build massive nests that supply sufficient insulation against the cold and help keep their early broods warm. And in accordance with the habits of many other species in which the female alone builds the nest and incubates the eggs, the male dances attendance upon his mate and escorts her, watching over her and guarding the territorial premises when she is at home. Courtship feeding plays an important role in the ceremonial rites of these two species, but during incubation, when the female subscribes to a very slow rhythm with extremely long sessions on the nest and rare and very short recesses, the feeding is turned into a ritual of practical necessity. The offerings brought by the male at this time no longer consist of just a piece of grit or a seed, as they did during courting days, but of a substantial porridge of mashed seeds served with all due ceremony on the nest or near it. And here the similarities between the two species end.

The red crossbill is a compact bird of decisive fluid movements. Its plumage has that structural stiffness shared by some of the larger finches, solid to the touch, rapping in sound when serried wing feathers beat the air. Rust-red in color, rather than rosy like the white-wing, the male displays no contrasting designs; only the edgings of his dark-brown or black feathers on wings and tail may at times be delicately tinted with red. The female is grayish-olive with a more or less intense wash of yellow over the head, sides, and rump; she shows no white on the wings and less striping on the back than the white-wing. Like the waxwings, the crossbills perch upright mainly because their legs are rather short. When they feed they crawl around like parrots from one cone to the other, using their curved crossed prying pincers to hang on while their feet change support.

The most intriguing feature of the modest pine siskin is surely the shape of its bill. Exquisitely curved and pointed, it is not given due credit in any illustration I have seen. It is the perfect tool for the small bird that relishes clinging like a bee to the conelike fruits of the alderbush and picking the seeds, in the process dropping some of them in the snow to mark the visit. The pine siskin's overall striped plumage in shades of brown and white is relieved by wing spots and tail flashes, lemon-yellow in about half of the birds and white in the rest, regardless of sex.

As to the pine siskin's voice, what comes out of that elegant little bill is far beyond anything suggested by the bird's modest appearance and unobtrusive ways. Here is a vocal Cinderella of amazing ability. The siskin is hardly ever silent. Even its simplest note is often protracted according to circumstances, improved, inflected no end. When a pair is together or a flock is assembled the birds communicate in an incessant flow of enchanting softly melodious notes. When in a singing mood the pine siskin outdoes himself, whether he performs at dawn or in the air or just sitting on a twig, half hidden among the green shadows of the conifers. And the recital he delivers is sustained longer than that of any other bird I have heard in this northern forest, songs full of trills, double notes, and soft liquid warbles occasionally interspersed with the harsher burry notes that distinguish the utterances of this species.

In early April I find the first nest of the red crossbills in a bushy pine standing on top of a rocky outcropping along the southwestern shore of Pimisi Bay. A few days later on the brow of the same elevated shoreline I find three other nests, two in bushy spruces and one in a tall red pine, a loose colony of red crossbill residences within three acres of land.

I know of no occupation so fullfilling as that of being a watcher. The observing self is pushed into the background, almost obliterated except for a cramped leg or an aching muscle imposed by enforced immobility. The present is dominated by the natural stage and all senses are focused upon the amazing events that are constantly taking place. Sensations and sounds arrange themselves into orderly sequences of action, revealing, mystifying, exciting, never lacking in interest, often sensational, sometimes spectacular in meaning and consequence.

As I reach the point where my own self-importance is left behind, but not before, the portals are flung open upon a strange and fascinating and extraordinarily law-abiding world full of reality and intimate life. All proportions change. I am aware of new dimensions extending far beyond the limits of the usual familiar very narrow sphere within which I was conscious only of the things directly connected with myself. I am still the center of things, but I am no longer able to touch the walls on all sides. I am out, far out, a small speck in an immense field. My own shrinkage brings a touch of illuminating humility that prevents me from meddling with things and from destroying the natural with my clumsy contact. The new attitude changes my perception substantially. I begin to grasp the unannounced event, the hitherto unrecognized detail, the important connection, the fluidity of natural interplay that exists between the different parts of this newly discovered environment. And as I gradually learn to distinguish and to pick out shape, light, color, and movement, the causes, the connections, the relationships and interdependencies within the whole begin to make sense and to impress me with their harmony and finely set balance.

So I sit still, absolutely still, and absorb what I can of the great play. I hear a tremendous splashing. Two deer are swimming across the bay coming this way, forging like two magnificent icebreakers through the slushy ice still floating on the surface of the partially defrosted lake. The noise they make fills the air. They land a scanty hundred feet from where I am motionless. A sweet southerly breeze blows my scent the other way. Stepping daintily on cloven hoofs they walk past close behind me, unperturbed, unsuspecting. The nearest one gives its head a mighty shake, an icy drop of water is catapulted unexpectedly onto my cheek. The deer climb the slope, they are in no hurry, the trees and the bushes swallow them.

How she came to be there and where she came from, I do not know. But suddenly out of the corner of my eye, I am aware of movement. I fix the spot and discern the weasel-like shape, lithe, elongated, clothed in smooth silky dark-brown mink fur, a white spot under the chin. The mink, obviously a female in the last stages of pregnancy, sees something that interests her, sniffs the air. But I remain motionless and she does not take alarm. Her head sinks down upon her front paws; her eyes are closed. She sleeps in a strip of sunshine eight feet from where I sit. The slightest movement on my part, a hardly perceptible turn of my head, starts her out of her slumber. Did she hear me? Can she see through closed eyes? Her triangular head shoots up; she is wide awake; her wet nose moves, sniffs. A red squirrel comes loping along, talking loudly to itself, entirely unaware of the mink. My heart flutters at my throat in anticipation of what may happen. The squirrel continues on its way, running along a log toward the mink, still unsuspecting. Suddenly, less than two feet from the mink's nose, the squirrel sees her, stops in its tracks, utters soft almost-whispered alarm notes. To fight or to flee, what is it going to be? The momentous decision is made lightning fast. The squirrel turns and precipitately departs, far more quietly than it came.

The mink must have been aware of the squirrel. The noise, the scent, the vibration of movement, she could hardly have avoided noticing, but she gives no sign. She remains in full repose, eyes closed or merely slitted. Then with great detachment she terminates her nap. She arises, slips behind a rock and onto a mossy log that leads to a small pool. She sits on the log and scratches herself with obvious delight, thoroughly, unhurriedly, then runs out of sight.

All this—the deer, the mink, the red squirrel—relates to the life of the crossbills in various ways, sometimes directly, at other times indirectly. All of them belong to this northern forest and their lives and their presence harmonize with the austerity of the spring-winter season and with the expectancy of the beginning of growth and new life.

The drifts are still deep on the northward slopes and the ice is floating on the lake and the frost in the night spreads a crisp crust over the patches of snow that the sun softened and melted during the day when the red crossbills start building their nest. They go to work at the right time, impulsively and with perfect insouciance, when the forest is full of the special kind of food on which they and their young thrive. Always the two birds, he and she, are together, almost inseparable. She arrives leading the way and carrying the gathered materials in her bill, he follows close behind and swoops down on a twig a little above the chosen site where she deposits her selected contribution in the densest part halfway up in the tall spruce. She carries green moss, bits of beard moss, and dead grasses to the nest. She flies to a cedar stick that leans against a rock just below the nest-branch where the storms of the winter placed it. She clings to the stick and tears off long strips of its pliable inner bark, trails them behind her to the nest. Meanwhile her mate sits, surrounded by greenery, and watches, his red breast reflecting the suffusion of color sent through the trees from the dazzling sunrise. He sings softly, seemingly in love with every note that escapes his bubbling throat. Off she flies again, her keen eye having espied a tuft of brown hairs shed by a deer and left stuck to a twig that scraped against the deer's side in passing. With it she lines the nest, turns around, molds it into a wadded warm repository for the eggs to come.

The incubation period is for the red crossbills a time of harmony and felicity. This early in the season the forest harbors few predators except blue jays and red squirrels. Few birds of their own kind with territorial pretensions are free to trespass and make trouble. The land is spacious; the crossbills' feeding areas extend far and wide, free and open to them all. Only the nest tree and its immediate surroundings need to be defended. This absence of provocation is greatly in their favor and leaves the birds in a state of inconspicuous quiet peacefulness.

In the concentrated effort to raise a family the attachment between the mates reaches its peak. Quite literally the female cannot live without the male and at the same time successfully incubate the eggs. In the chilly early spring season the eggs require very close attention and a steady generous gift of warmth to develop normally. In a neat division of labor the male takes upon himself the duties of chief provider of food, while the female is left wholly in charge of the eggs. She leaves them for only the briefest recesses three or four times a day and at night she sleeps on them.

From a distant foraging ground the male arrives home in bouncing high flight across the lake, his bill, throat, and gullet full of mashed seeds. Listen! I hear him calling and the female hears him too. She lifts her head and sits in an attitude of tense listening. She knows his voice and unfailingly distinguishes his calls from those of every other crossbill that flies over the top of her tree. She never makes a mistake. She responds to his calling. She begins to murmur a continuous tirade of babyish notes, *chetititit*, softly at first, then, as the male approaches, gradually louder and louder until her voice rises in an excited vibrating crescendo. The next instant he is beside her and peers down at her through the green screening, every feather on his head, neck, and body sleeked and flattened in a display of congeniality. He places his crossed bill sideways to hers and smothers her notes with his offering of food, adds more twice, eight times, a godly meal. Highly excited, she accepts, wings trembling and tail aloft. As her mate withdraws she subsides upon the nest and the two resume their interrupted conversation. For as long as he remains close to her, preening and resting, their exchange of notes continues, as it always goes on and on when they are together during the whole of their nesting season.

The eggs in the nest hatch in due course. But the event does not at first cause many changes in the crossbills' daily routines. Except for the female's recesses when they go off to the feeding grounds together, the male still forages alone and brings food to the female. She accepts as if it were meant for her, with wings fluttering and baby-bird utterances. But she does not swallow it. She rises and with her eyes large and shining and the feathers on her head smoothed so that it looks sleek and thin, she peers down under her breast. Three chalices, resembling the red fringed blossoms of sweet williams, open before her and to them she gives all the food that her mate brought.

At the age of about four or five days, when the nestlings' eyes begin to open and their pinfeathers to sprout, the necessity of brooding them lessens. With that a change occurs in the parents' daily program and the female joins her mate more frequently to help gather food for the young. Always arriving back slightly ahead of the male, she feeds the young first and cleans the nest. He waits, watches, then steps forward to fulfill his part of the transaction, and the fare of the young is the same as the female received, a porridge of seeds. Two weeks pass and the thriving nestlings are now fully feathered. They begin to prepare for the nest-leaving ceremony. They rise on oversized feet and flap their wings. They carry on a continuous chatter, as the female did when she behaved like a baby bird and was fed by her mate.

The seventeenth day of the nestling period dawns mild and overcast. The snow is all gone and the ice went out of the lake several days ago. There is no wind and sound carries far in the stillness. The female calls from the top of the nest tree. She is tense, her movements are short and abrupt. Slowly she begins to descend from one branch to the next. By her behavior I know something is wrong, but I see nothing, hear nothing untoward. The male replaces the female in the top of the tree and gives his resonant call and everybody knows where he is. The female continues her descent, one branch at a time. Why all this wariness? What are the birds so worried about? The female beats her wings against her sides, calls. And then, just as she alights on the branch next to the nest, a blue jay calls loudly.

So that was it! Quickly the female leaves the vicinity of the nest. I hear her soft warning note: *lu—lu—lu!* The two crossbills fly into a tree at some distance from the nest and sit there together, watching, calling loudly.

At that very second the blue jay alights on a branch just below the nest. The heavenly blue bird with its crest on end and its flowing tail half open stretches its neck to see better, pulling its black necklace all out of shape. What is the jay looking for? What does it know about this neighborhood, predacious as it is on occasion? I cannot wait to find out and scream foolishly. The blue jay quickly departs and the crossbills cease calling. All fly away, everything is quiet, and all happening is suspended temporarily.

The crossbills return and again the female flies into the nest tree while the male waits in another one. She calls softly, bats her wings nervously as she circles around the nest without going into it. Then for a fleeting second she perches on the rim with her head feathers erected, looks into it. The nest is empty.

As the female leaves, the male visits the nest, looks into it, finds nothing. But led by a sound from a thick clump of branchlets beside the nest he finds one of the young birds. He feeds it, gives it all he carries, and afterward, even in this stressful moment, mechanically cleans up around the tiny fledgling. Once again the female flies into the top of the nest tree and gives her warning note.

Sure enough, the blue jay is back on the very branch around which the young are hidden after they apparently burst from the nest at the blue jay's first visitation. Let the blue jay get its dinner at the feeding station! I cannot bear to see the sacrifice of the young crossbills and I chase it away.

Peace reigns once again. Guided by their subdued chatter, the father finds each of the three fledglings scattered among the green branchlets and feeds them all. But the female continues to be upset. She neglects the young, flies about, calls, alights in the top of the nest tree, bats her wings, flies away, and then repeats these maneuvers over and over again, as if the absence of the blue jay was not yet an actuality. All her well-coordinated activities are entirely out of gear and it takes her a long time to regain her composure sufficiently to fall in with the male's continued, uninterrupted attendance upon their miraculously surviving trio.

The following day I find the whole family intact in a cedar thicket by the lake not far from the nest tree. The young are very small and I have no difficulty catching one of them. Its plumage, I note, is slate-gray and heavily striped, rendering the little bird almost invisible against the mottled background of the earth and the moss and the trees unless it betrays itself by movement. Light-colored natal down still clings to its shoulders and to the top of its head and its light gray bill is not yet long enough for the tips to cross. Stubby-tailed and so young, is it not too soon out of its moss-built hair-lined nest? At that point the crossbills' soft alarm notes interrupt my observations. Again the blue jay is at the nest searching for the cheap meal that, luckily, is no longer there but nestled warmly and safely here in my hand. Where is a small living thing like this ever secure?

It is strange that the blue jay did not return sooner but delayed until today, after the family had moved away from the neighborhood of the nest. Yesterday the blue jay would have had a good chance of success, for the crossbills would scarcely have been able to persuade these fledglings prematurely out of the nest to follow them over even so short a distance as to this grove without much time-consuming tempting and fussing. In my absence the blue jay would probably not have failed to carry out its predacious intent. Persistence is the hallmark of survival, granted the fittest and the smartest. But in this case the blue jay's timing was bad both before and after the critical period. Had it been a day earlier in locating the nest, the nestlings would have been incapable of exploding to safety under the green branchlets. Now their instinctive act worked and, being activated at exactly the right moment, how beautifully it compensated for the parents' unwillingness or inability to prevent the blue jay's nest-robbing attempt! One may look for the cause of the parents' seeming inefficacy partly in their reliance, developed through the ages, upon the nest's safety under sufficient cover, and partly in the timing of the blue jay's assault. The behavior patterns of the parents constantly undergo subtle adjustments according to changing circumstances and when the young reach a certain age and acquire a certain mobility, the attitude of the parents is recast for the nest-leaving act. At this stage the nest has served its purpose and the necessity for its active defense has disappeared.

The safety of the young crossbills, however, was brought about with no guarantee for the future. The forced and certainly slightly premature emergence of these young birds into the open environment has reduced their chances of survival. The balance of nature tips this way and that with scant regard for single individual lives but only for the overall continuity.

I returned to the cedar grove again the next day to look for the family, but I could not find them. I searched as far and wide as I deemed the tiny birds could reasonably have been expected to move. But the place was dead. The birds were gone, and I do not know how or where they went.

They navigate in the ethereal element like the heavier-than-air machine which maneuvers by power and impetus. They cruise in deep elegant dips and upswings, but to escape the charging predator they dart away heedlessly like feathered projectiles. They fight like wrestlers, using a technique of interlocking beaks instead of arms and necks, and like wrestlers they incline toward a ponderous demeanor. Such are the evening grosbeaks.

Among the finches the evening grosbeak is one of the most striking in appearance as well as behavior. The male's plumage gives the general impression of a yellow bird with a black tail; the wings are black too with the exception of a large area of white that shows prominently in flight as in repose. The lovely warm brown color of the head and neck blends into the clear yellow of the body. Across the forehead he wears a well-defined band of golden feathers that extends from eye to eye and a little beyond. These features are important in his courtship behavior, as we shall see. The female is dove-gray but the tips of her feathers on neck and sides are tinted yellow. She also has a black tail and wings, but in her they are decorated with a pearly design in white that varies greatly with the individual in extent and form and provides a beautiful display in flight and, more important still, in certain significant courtship attitudes and movements.

The evening grosbeak, so the books tell us, is originally a western species. Only quite recently, after 1910, these birds began turning up in the eastern part of the continent in gradually increasing numbers.

Unlike the crossbills and the pine siskin, the evening grosbeak is not a truly nomadic species, although its appearances sometimes seem to form patterns of erratic peregrinations. Its young are raised on insects and the breeding season must therefore coincide with the time of the year when this kind of food is available. Hence the breeding season of the evening grosbeak is at a set time; here at Pimisi Bay it begins in May and ends in July or

August. This regularity encourages the establishment of habitual breeding grounds to which the birds tend to return in the spring every year. In this sense the evening grosbeak is a true migrant.

The northern coniferous forests and the mixed forest ecotones seem to meet the nesting requirements of the evening grosbeak best. Here the bird finds good nest sites in the bushy top branches of the tall evergreens, a place it seems to favor over many other sites it is known to have occupied. Here, too, in these forests abide plenty of insects of the kind the grosbeak likes, among which is the spruce budworm whose outbreaks at times attract great numbers of grosbeaks to the affected areas. To the adult bird the forest offers seeds of various kinds, the buds of poplar and birch, wild fruits such as juneberries, cherries, and many others, upon which it depends for a large part of its food. As to its territorial habits, the evening grosbeak subscribes to the same rules as the true nomadic species. Gregarious by nature, it often nests in loose colonies and the territory it defends is only the immediate surroundings of the nest tree. Like the crossbills, the evening grosbeak also travels considerable distances from the nesting place to forage. Once a store burned down a few miles from Pimisi Bay and bags of salt melted and drained into the coarse gravel of the yard. For at least three breeding seasons several scores of evening grosbeaks nesting in the forests all around visited this place from the time they arrived in the spring until after their young fledged, to pick the salty gravel and the charcoal from the burned timbers.

When the nesting season is at an end, family groups of evening grosbeaks join one another and the flocks largely abandon the deep forest and begin to wander. At this time the birds develop a strong liking for the seeds of the Manitoba maple, the box elder, mainly, I believe, because birds, like people, are usually attracted by the easiest pickings, and they flock into the parks, the cities, and the villages where these trees are planted for their ornamental value. Here the birds stay and eat until all the seeds are devoured and the last samara is flung away before they leave in search of the next bonanza. Similarly any winter feeding station that the birds encounter en route receives their close attention. But in spite of these artificial attractions, the abundance of the local supply of natural foods is the condition which determines the birds' final move, whether they stay on or not.

As fall turns into winter the sexes tend to separate so that the flocks remaining closer to the breeding grounds consist mostly of males, while the females, more prone to travel, are found at greater distances away. This tendency gives the observer a good indication of the likely extension of the evening grosbeaks' winter movements in any given year. The probabilities of an invasion into the regions farther south are good when the females disappear from the Pimisi Bay areas and the transient and wintering flocks there consist mostly of males. But in the years when the flocks here are larger and the sexes mixed, the chances are that the natural food supply in the north is ample and the birds will not travel very far.

In late March or early April, sometimes even later, a sudden influx of females often heralds the grosbeaks' return migration to the breeding grounds. The arriving birds alight in the trees and sit. Presently they fly down, spread over the partly bare forest floor to pick the samaras of the soft maples that dropped last autumn and lay well preserved under the snow all winter. The forest rings with the birds' incessant almost deafening *chip-churr*ing chorus, extensively varied now in the early spring, each bird making its contribution to the general singsong about every other second or so. No one is silent; they call as they sit, as they hop, as they eat. The husks fall from each side of the powerful bills that are now about to lose the bone-colored cover they bear during the non-breeding season; with the approach of spring and courtship the bill of the evening grosbeak turns a resplendent apple-green color. To find oneself in the midst of such a lively and vociferous company is an amazing experience of sound and sight.

When Dusky, the male evening grosbeak, discovered the close connection that existed between the chickadees, the sunflower seed, and me, he became greatly interested. He came flying, perched on a low branch at a little distance, and from there observed how the chickadees demanded and got their due ration. A few days later he made an abortive attempt to alight on my hand, but halfway there he turned quickly and dashed back to the perch and safety. That, however, was all it took to induce him to fulfill his intention. The next moment he sat on my hand and the husks fell from his bill as he picked and ate seed after seed with complete deliberation. After that, espying me from afar, he flew to meet me. When he saw me inside the house, he sometimes tried to fly through the window pane which he could not see and in the attempt knocked his large bill against it. I took the hint my own way and Dusky got his seeds, though not by crashing the gate.

Dusky's approach to my hand is always direct and silent. He is a bird large and bright enough not to be overlooked. But like the chickadees, as he lands he never fails to indicate the wild bird's perennial distrust and insecurity, its most effective life-saving attributes, by uttering his soft alert note, *chou— chou—chou.* Thereupon he gains confidence quickly and begins to call in loud *chip-chur*ring tones which inform his fellows of his whereabouts.

The gregariousness of the evening grosbeak is unfailing and in response to Dusky's calls a small crowd assembles. The birds alight in the surrounding trees and open an animated musical *chip-churr* conversation, an enchanting avian dissertation on togetherness that obviously is reassuring to them all. One male alights on my shoulder, another on my hand opposite Dusky. Dusky's only reaction to this close company is to eat faster. The area of individual distance in the evening grosbeak does not extent beyond the reach of its bill, so that, for a while, the situation retains its atmosphere of blithe neutrality—until a female alights beside Dusky.

Immediately Dusky takes exception, not to the presence of the female at all, but to the male beside him. He flings himself at the innocent bystander. Their stout bills interlock and the two wrestle, pushing the female off my hand. But the battle claims all their attention. It increases in intensity and both birds fall overboard. That stops the fighting, because willy-nilly they separate on their way down and, with a space opening between them, their drive to fight evaporates.

Now it is the middle of March. The nights are cold and frosty, but the sap is running, induced by the increasing heat of the sun in the middle of the day. Several flocks of evening grosbeaks arrive directly from the roost and assemble in the tall poplars at the edge of the forest. There they sit and call, each bird adding its voice to this imperious communicative exhilarating morning concert. Among them is Dusky.

Hardly moving, for well on an hour the grosbeaks just sit there and call. The deliberate leisurely formality is the evening grosbeaks' specialty. In one tree there are only males, in another only females, in one or two others the sexes are mixed. Occasionally a male and a female take off at the same time, fly together for a short while, and then alight and sit together. Other pairs perform the same maneuver, some of them several times. But their performance of these activities gives me no true indication that their separation into pairs is either serious or lasting. The main theme of the current moment still seems to be the assembly and the chorus.

The next time I find Dusky he is again with a flock sitting in the trees and feeding on buds with great concentration. But on this occasion the flock is composed of an equal number of males and females. I detect also another significant change. The birds are doing no loud calling; their conversation is conducted in half-whispered very musical notes that sound something like *chouwee-chouwee-chouwee* repeated over and over again.

Meantime the weather gets milder and the snow disappears. Once again the lake is full of movement and—when there is no wind—of beautiful reflections with gray and mauve overtones. The first warm days of spring make it easy for us to forget that the hepaticas were not always there decorating the slope in front of the house and opening their faces to the sun, that the mourning mantles ever stopped fluttering along their erratic paths, that the brown needles shed from the pines last autumn were not forever sun-warmed and fragrant. The grosbeaks are not insensible to the subtle change.

Dusky no longer takes any notice of me. The flocks dissolve and the evening grosbeaks break up into smaller companies of three or four, some of them into pairs whose tête-à-têtes I sometimes indiscreetly surprise here and there in a secluded green corner. The males are growing notably short-tempered and fight more often among themselves, but they pick no quarrels with the females.

I am not surprised one day to find Dusky in the company of two females. One of them hops toward him along the branch upon which he perches. She engages in a spectacular display directed at Dusky. It consists of highly accentuated rhythmic pivoting movements in which she presents to him first her left, then her right side. Her fanned tail with its pearly design in black and white swishes to and fro, her apple-green bill points upward at a jaunty angle, and she bobs her head up and down, from side to side, in tempo with the pivoting movements. Her performance is all challenge, the exuberant female offering herself at a price.

Rapidly becoming prey to mounting excitement at the sight of her sister's display, the second female too begins bobbing her head up and down and gives vent to a series of loud emphatic notes, *shirrr—shirrr—shirrr*. From this she goes over to a pivoting act of her own, also directed at Dusky, with her tail swishing magnificently from side to side.

So far Dusky has remained passive and neutral, but the arrival of another male fills him with excitement. The two males immediately engage in a bill-locking bout, with Dusky trying his best to displace the unwanted intruder. Neither activity lasts long because the mood of courting is too strongly upon them. Instead all four birds enter into a session of mutual displays whose most prominent feature is the pivoting act executed by both sexes. And I soon realize that what I am witnessing is the first stage of the evening grosbeaks' pair formation.

A day or so later I chance upon the next installment of the courtship rituals. This time only two birds are present, he and she. In a horizontal line from bill tip to tail tip, the male stretches his body toward the female. His wings, half extended and vibrating violently, show prominently the gleaming white wing patch. He sings—and few have ever heard the song of the evening grosbeak, for he is a caller and not a singer by habit. The new and the rare in nature require sharp attention to avoid misinterpretation. For all its slightly slurred quality, this song is loud and remarkably silvery. It consists of a highly musical sequence of warbled and whistled notes, amazingly varied, that lasts and lasts and lasts. Singing, the male moves toward the female almost hesitatingly. As he reaches her she grasps his bill with hers and something, I do not know what, passes from bill to bill. The contact lasts but a second and she turns away.

A little later the birds go to a feeder together and the female picks a sunflower seed and tenders it to him. She does this twice, and twice he accepts. Later the roles are reversed and this time the male offers the female a piece of grit. From then on courtship feeding seems to become the male's prerogative entirely. And as it increases in frequency the female cancels her previous pose of challenge and passes briefly through a stage of seeming indifference. Finally she is ready to accept his symbolic offerings with growing eagerness and, playing the submissive fledgling not yet able to feed itself, she creeps up to her mate begging with her beak wide open and her wings trembling.

I do not hear the song of the male again. Their courtship has entered upon a new stage in which the female no longer performs her pivoting rites. Their partnership is recognized and is now being confirmed. She is the neutral figure, the object, and lives within a narrowly delineated sexual territory protected and defended by the male. He is the principal actor and her mere nearness is enough to throw him into a state of vibrating excitement. Slowly he erects the brown feathers on head and neck so that these parts appear hugely enlarged. The bright yellow eyebrow line stands on end and like a golden coronet crowns his forehead. His black tail tilts at a conspicuous upward angle. Except for the bouffant head and neck, the feathers on the rest of his body are sleeked down so that his posterior part looks very thin. His wings, held curved out from his sides

[117]

with their tips almost trailing, quiver strongly. With mincing steps he moves in front of the female, presenting her a frontal view of himself. He sways like a top at full motion.

The female is too busy to pay much attention to these frivolities. She tears at a tough rootlet and throws her weight upon it. The male in front of her continues his impassioned display, swaying, swaying. He picks up a loose rootlet, manipulates it gently in his bill, then drops it. When the female gets a small collection gathered in her bill she hops around and picks up odd bits left lying and then flies with the load in a beeline to a tall white pine near the water's edge. Seeing her go, the male instantly changes his role to that of a normal-looking escort and quickly catches up to her. In the five-pronged crotch of one of the topmost branches she deposits her burden, sits on it, molds it with her body. Their continuous exchange of soft notes, *chouwee-chouwee*, are borne on the light breeze to where I stand watching them.

Did I by this time entertain any doubt about the evening grosbeaks' ability to recognize each other personally, an accident provides me with the conclusive proof. The appearance of a hawk scatters a group at the feeder, and one of them, a female, smashes against our window. She drops to the ground, flutters weakly a few feet, falls on her side, and lies there motionless. Seeing her drop, the male flies to her and goes into full display beside her prostrate body.

Thinking she may still be alive, I pick her up and bring her inside. The usual treatment for knocked-out birds, a cold head bath and confinement in darkness, soon brings her around and after an hour's rest she is ready to be released.

The male is still in the very same place where I left him after I picked up the female, sitting like a statue in a void of inactivity, obviously not having moved since he lost sight of his mate. His attitude suggests traumatic shock. All around him grosbeaks of both sexes travel busily to and from the feeders, but he takes no notice of them. As the female, his own, leaves my hand and flies out to mingle with the crowd, the male immediately recognizes her and her alone among the many, springs to life, and flies out to her. When they meet he falls back a wingbeat or two behind her and in a wide circle the two fly together to the tall pine by the lake.

CHAPTER SEVEN

The Miracle of the Returned Bird

The autumnal sky is blue-black and studded with stars, alive with light shooting in trembling shafts across immense distances in how many lightyears? A deep awareness of this universe, mysterious because of its dimensions so far beyond the earth's limits, so far beyond anything my wildest thought can grasp in its intense glittering reality, is heavy upon me. An exultant feeling of being a part of this limitless world is coessential with this awareness, a part nonetheless valid, however infinitesimal, because of my having evolved out of the very same mold with the very same character of change and evanescence. At this moment this vast expanse appears to be of an affinity so encompassing as to be almost tangible. I can reach out and almost touch the stillness, the air, the muffled sounds, and the starlight. The passing night unaffected by the day's contaminations is an enormously satisfying reality.

Perhaps in this idea is to be found the answer to the question of why migrating birds so often fly by night. Might not the de-

tachment from the earth and the entrance into an environment
of enormous spaciousness and visibility even at night, or at least
the sensation of it, give to the birds' night flight that special
buoyancy which is required to sustain them in the air for hours
over great distances while the forests, the mountains, meadows,
lakes, rivers, and seas down below are lost to them? Might it
not give them a sense of almost inviolate security which daylight and the closer contact with the earth never provides?
Were I in imagination to put myself in the place of the birds,
the night is certainly the time I would choose to fly amid the
stars, through or above the transparencies of the clouds in a
medium of nothing that supports me as on a pillar of distance
from the earth.

The coming of light begins to tint the edge of the horizon
with a suffusion of roseate illumination that intensifies with
each passing minute. From the space above come faint voices.
Bird is calling to bird, never waiting for an answer. Their notes
repeated at set intervals trace the course of each bird, threads of
communication spun between them invisibly, keeping them
within earshot of one another and keeping them apart species
from species, one bird not too close to the next. They fly on a
broad front and their voices give them away, some sounding
loudly from overhead, others coming fainter and fainter from
far out over the lake. On this morning of strong migratory
movement, these birds having passed overhead, disappear leaving no trace, and another wave of nightly aviators follows in
their wake. But then, dropping their *beeps* upon the air in a rising crescendo, a flock of birds sweeps in from the north. Suddenly all noise ceases. They have landed. Silent and still, invisible though they are, I sense their presence in the tops of the
trees, on the branches. Leaning against the trunk of a towering
pine, I hold my breath lest a single one of their notes escape
me.

During their interval of quiescence after landing I wait and I
wonder what the birds are doing while the light is still too dim

to tempt them to move. Are they really there, all those birds whose calls so positively gave them away but that now seem to be swallowed by the silence? Are they resting, preening, sleeping?

Slowly, inch by inch, daylight creeps in over the land. It touches first the tops of the trees, then penetrates between the trunks down into the undergrowth to play upon the forest floor in illuminated patches. This is the signal and once again bird begins calling to bird. The sound of their voices tells me where they are though I still cannot see them. Snatches of song mingle with the call-notes, lighthearted outbursts of inconsequential glee, casually suggesting the propriety of maintaining individual distance in an emotional situation. The effusions of some of the performers are given in the clear self-assertive versions of the formal song patterns whereby they reveal their identities. The songs of others are sometimes slightly distorted in presentation, sometimes abbreviated, often hoarsely pronounced as if the songster had just regained a voice lost temporarily or as if it had not yet learned the musical lesson of its own species. And I am left puzzled: who is the originator of the unorthodox ditty?

The sun still loiters below the horizon. Mists form and rise in trailing veils along the waterways and envelop the shores. Along the eastern horizon a strong light spreads slowly. It illuminates the waterdrops suspended in the mist and makes them appear like infinitely delicate lacework. Then from out of the pink-tinted vapors the hills across the lake spring into view, bluish-gray and shadowy, footless as if detached from their bases and lifted into the air above the mists. The amazing illusion lingers, enhanced by the beams of the rising sun playing upon the mists from behind. And all nature bathes in the enchantment of its own creation. Then, as suddenly as it appeared, the picture dissolves. The mists close like curtains released from the wings of the stage. It starts to rain, an intimate chilly shower presaging the coming of colder weather.

Day has arrived and the birds are moving. A branchlet shakes lightly, a leaf trembles, as a bird alights or takes off and the pliant support is released from its airy weight. To recognize, even to catch sight of every flitting member of this early morning concentration of migrants is impossible. My ears are not sharp or perceptive enough to hear each message passed from bird to bird. I must be content to trace a dash of color, a half defined form, before they vanish again, and by a process of elimination to assign a tentative name to the fleeting apparition until with luck a second look provides a chance of positive identification. I must be satisfied with recognizing two out of ten of them and from the multitudinous impressions that crowd upon my senses attempt to write with only a semblance of accuracy a record of the presence and behavior of this throng of light-winged travelers.

The flock of migrants drifts along the shore onto the narrow tip of a small promontory. I wait to see them wing their way easily across the strip of water, less than a thousand feet wide, that separates this land from the Peninsula. But the birds stop as if in front of a barrier. They assemble in the tall trees, they do not feed, they do not even rest, but sit there and look as if they were waiting for something to happen.

A long minute passes. Then with straggly crest on end and sounding its loud rattling call, a kingfisher sweeps in upon the scene. It flies out over the lake but the next instant turns back defeated. Why hesitate to cross a width of water which this bird of determined movements and loud noises, no stranger to water, must have braved innumerable times in less than three fast wing-beats? What odd objection, contagious as a disease, is paralyzing the initiative of all these birds? The kingfisher makes several more sallies out over the water, only to turn back. Then all at once, without obvious cause, its reluctance evaporates and it shoots down to the surface of the water and across, then swoops on to a dead branch on the other side. Another loud rattling call echoes across the water, a flash of blue, and the kingfisher disappears from sight.

The robins, the flickers, and the warblers watch the maneuvers of the kingfisher with keen interest. Its conquest of the crossing provides the necessary stimulus to take them out of the trance and they begin moving about in the trees. Two robins take off, fly out over the water, but break off midway and turn back. Once more they launch themselves into the air, once again hesitation gets the better of them. Their abortive attempts to cross occupy two more minutes, and by this time I share in full measure the frustration obviously affecting the birds. At that moment one of the robins flings itself into the air out over the water, reaches the other side by the impulse of some mysterious force, and disappears among the trees.

This is the signal for the flock to take action. They have been held back long enough. The mood of every bird in sight changes abruptly, tension dissolves, and the robin's successful flight drives the crowd of them across the water in a long drawn-out stream. High in the air, their wings flapping, the rest of the robins fly in a straight line right across, the flickers lift on clapping wings and then scoot over, all sails folded; the small birds flit across the water like leaves detached in a big windstorm. At long last they have conquered the insignificant obstacle, the nonexistent obstacle, and leave it behind forgotten.

In a strangely acute way I am constantly aware of these birds moving in tireless throngs at the height of the season. Quite different from the large spectacular flights of the hawks and the geese, the movements of the small perching birds are for the most part unobtrusive, sometimes secretive, at other times unexpectedly overflowing into a limited area, a wave of birds that vanishes as it came, suddenly. Soon I learn to find the small scattered groups and the places they favor along creeks and rivers, along the ridges of the landscape, or through openings in the forest from whence they later emerge to follow a guiding feature of the land. On occasion I find them in large and exciting concentrations on a slope and along a particular wayside, or in some special place that boasts a temporary abundance of fruits or berries. The migrating bird is the plaything of a variety of environmental conditions—the wind, the clouds, the sun, the stars, and the relative warmth or coolness of the air. No two days present the same migratory picture, no two gatherings of birds act in the same way. I am continuously confronted with the changing theme, and these changes provide me the best chances to learn approximately how many and what kind of birds are on the move and what forces are at play for or against them.

I am in the midst of a gay stream of confusing fall warblers that have molted the brightly distinctive nuptial plumages by which they were so easily identified in the spring. Desperately I try to put the right names to at least a few of them. Two attract my special attention, two very similar birds, both yellow below and olive-green above. If my suspicion is right, one is a very common little bird and the other a very rare one. Is it the rare one? The excitement of the rarity never fails, and for the next half minute I am luckier than I have been before, for the two are together before me to be easily compared. From its size, the length of its soft yellow undertail coverts, the unbroken light-colored ring that encircles its eye. I am able for the first time positively to identify the long-looked-for Connecticut warbler. A bird primarily of the west and the central continental forests, occasionally it passes through our region in small numbers during migration, more often in the spring than in the fall when it is easily overlooked. Its companion, the mourning warbler, is one of my favorites, destined to flit across the pages of another chapter.

The sound of wild alarm cries startles me. Quick as thought the warblers dash for cover low down near the ground under the thick shelter of bracken and sarsaparilla, neither heeding nor fearing the proximity of me and my feet. The assault comes fast as lightning. The dark shadow streaks past the corner of my right eye, and I do not fully realize what is happening until I see the sharp-shinned hawk land on the rounded boulder.

Under its talons a tuft of soft yellow feathers trembles in a last spasmodic shudder. The weight of the hawk almost instantly suffocates the hapless one.

Do not disturb or distract the hawk, do not cause it to falter! What is to be done should be done fast; there is mercy in speed and surprise. For a moment the hawk remains sitting where it landed, its deep orange eye surveying the surroundings, a proud denizen of the forest pursuing its legitimate prey. Presently the hawk lifts easily, for the tiny limp burden is light, to perform the last rite elsewhere.

Almost two minutes pass and the small birds are still in hiding, invisible. One flushes under my feet, suddenly aware of the precarious neighborhood, but ducks back quickly under the bracken again. I wait for the next sign of life and after a little some of them begin to move warily, unobtrusively. Two or three fly up and depart swiftly as arrows. Trembling leaves reveal the hiding places of others. Surreptitiously they come out from cover and move on, one and then another. For a while the behavior of the birds is markedly subdued and their voices are silent. But gradually the resilience with which nature endows its creatures brings the flock back into its earlier state of zest and insouciance. Forgotten is the danger, the tragedy if such it were; left is but a net memory of the frightening experience to serve them in a future emergency by increasing their skill in self-preservation.

Today it is still warm, although a little cooler than yesterday, and the wind has turned east. Yesterday the movement of migrating birds was quite remarkable in certain well-traveled places, a hardwood ridge pointing southward and ending in a gully, a swampy meadow overgrown by willows, alders, highbush cranberries and isolated umbrella-shaped elms. Speed distinguished the flights. The birds were in an unusual hurry, hardly giving themselves time to stop, and snatching most of their food en route.

Something seems to be afoot, a change in the weather most likely, not yet a reality but just impending. Outside on the lawn I look at the sky. One and then another bird flies overhead southward and I recognize them by their call-notes as white-throated sparrows. After a while the number increases sharply and a few minutes later birds are shooting like comets across the open space of sky overhead. Soon there is a veritable stream of birds that goes on and on, hundreds of them, all white-throated sparrows, streaking across the sky and into the trees beyond, never stopping, flying on from tree to tree, from bush to bush. This stream of birds occupies a strip of forest several hundred feet wide from the lakeshore up the southeastern slope. One relay of birds is relieved by the next oncoming throng. The air is filled with the sound of their call-notes, a chorus of uninterrupted music because the number of throats producing it is so great.

Ordinarily this kind of migration close to the surface of the earth is conducted in a leisurely manner, with the birds giving themselves ample time to feed and to rest and even to stop over for a day or two where the food supply is good. But today this is not the case. Today the birds are in a tremendous hurry and I wonder what is driving them southward at such an inordinate speed. By this time the white-throats have acquired a following of other birds, swarms of warblers, creepers, nuthatches, hangers-on picked up along the way, birds just on the verge of starting on their long journey, requiring only the final incentive such as the sight of this passing fast-moving crowd to set them, too, going. And the migration of all these birds rolls on as a snowball rolls down the hill and increases in volume.

For more than an hour the birds keep coming, an unending stream of birds. How many? I cannot tell. How far does this snake of birds hugging the lakeshore and the ridges extend from head to tail? Neither before nor after this memorable September day have I seen so concentrated and so hurried a flight of migrating songbirds in these regions. Never have I seen so many white-throated sparrows together in one place. And much I doubt that these shores will ever see it again, for the birds no longer exist in such multitudes.

Finally the flight has passed and nothing but the wind from the east is moving in the trees. In the early hours of the following day the wind suddenly turns north and sweeps a sharp cold front across the Pimisi Bay region.

Long before the snow goes away, long before the ice is due to break up into large soggy chunks that float over the dam and crash to pieces in the rapids below, long before the first birds return from the south, a remarkable day dawns that gives promise of spring. There is on this day a special quality in the tepid sunshine that suggests better things to come, an extraordinary softness of the midwinter air that seems to forecast the time when the trees will burst into leaf and when the scent of the new leaves and of a thousand blossoms still fast asleep within their armour of unopened bracts will be heavy upon the air. The illusion fills me with anticipatory delight. It is impossible to desist from carrying the fanciful thought still further, to dream of full-blown cherry blossoms and their heavy-headed stamens trembling under burdens of yellow pollen, and with imagination running wild my ears fill with the music of a thousand birds, their voices swelling into an antiphony of birdsong. In the midst of winter with the land still under a thick cover of snow and the frost deep in the ground, spring on this day foreshadows its own inevitable arrival.

The turning point is reached, the worst is over. Winter begins to lose its grip on the land and each day brings its end nearer. The sun is beginning to work on the snow from above and its reflected glow acts upon it from below, slowly shrinking the white mass. Its heat forms around the trunks of the trees, deep swirled hollows that grow larger and deeper with every cloudless day.

Some of the chickadees that supported themselves at the feeding station during the winter are already beginning to leave for their nesting areas. Those that remain are singing. Their clear trebled notes predominate among the sounds that break the dawn silence. The blue jays are introducing into their conversations a variety of new utterances not heard since last summer and during the first part of the day the forest rings with their new vociferous ejaculations. This increased loquacity ushers in a new stage in the blue jays' breeding activities. The actual start occurred as far back as the latter part of December when their formation into pairs was ratified by the delicate rite of courtship feeding. But that is as far as they got and during the following months emphasis was strongly on survival. With the approach of spring a new need arises, that of increased segregation. This, naturally, brings with it sharpened social relations against encroachment and interference, to which the blue jays are now giving expression in their new vocal repertoire.

The increasing glow of the sun alternating with heavy night frosts creates a hard crust all over the forest. Where travel during the winter was impossible without snowshoes, now comes the time when the snow supports one for a wonderful brief interval before the spring thaw arrives. In the morning before the sun has time to soften the crust I am off. I run over the gleaming snow with the greatest of ease. I slide down the hills sitting on my heels. The roughest recesses of the wilderness lie open to me. I get into steep places, into dark places where I seldom or never was before, into places where the tracks of the hares, the deer, the ruffed grouse, the foxes, and the wolves have printed telltale sequences of recent undisturbed and exciting events.

Two night-black ravens sail slowly across the tops of the trees uttering gruff noises, the pair that nests on the ledge above the river. They turn their heads and their large slightly curved beaks this way and that. What are they looking for, these opportune garbage collectors of nature's?

Over the brow of a hill I come unexpectedly upon three

deer. They do not see me and I stay motionless with the wind blowing gently in my face. Frightened by something behind them which I cannot see they go suddenly, white flags flying. They dash straight at the place where I am, catch sight of me in the last split second, and veer sideways, two to the right and one to the left. Without even a snort they dash past me and I feel the wind from their fleeing bodies lightly fanning my face. That was a close one; it leaves me almost breathless.

A while later I come out on the top of the high cliffs along the river. Below, narrow streaks of inky water predict the impending break-up of the ice. On the other side, above the rust-colored cliffs crowned by a fringy hat of evergreens, the blue-gray hills spread their panoramic contours into the distance. Two red foxes lope side by side across the ice at the mouth of the river and vanish among the bushes on the far shore. One of them reappears a moment later and returns the same way it came. Ever so often it stops, looks back and emits a quavering howl, *wrraaaoouw*. Its mate's answering howl echoes against the rock walls of the river. This performance is repeated half a dozen times until the first fox reaches shore just below where I am standing. In its own good time the mate finally emerges and trots across the ice at a leisurely pace. Two herring gulls, enticed by the opening water of the river and scouting for something to eat, spot the fox. Sensing the menace by instinct or from memory, the gulls dive upon the animal, once, three times, screaming at the top of their voices, their wings flapping, pink feet trailing, and bills pointed downward. But the fox nimbly sidesteps its attackers, and in so doing it runs perilously near the edge of the water. I hold my breath—is it going to fall in, is the ice worn thin by the dark current going to break? But the ice carries, the fox escapes its worriers, and the herring gulls float away on set wings and disappear, two gleaming white specks against the blue hills. A third fox howls, but its singing does not last and silence envelops the scene once again.

A soft wind is blowing from the south, caressing the trees, the rocks, and my cheek. The water of the lake is rising; the ice is lifted upon its broad back and breaks away from the shores with melancholy tinkling noises. Long tongues of dark open water push out from the river's mouth into the middle of the lake. Back in the bush, out along the highway, the water begins to sing softly. The ringing notes of two or three evening grosbeaks mingle with the water's song as they fly over. Over yonder a pine siskin circles above its perched mate and elaborates its emotions in a ravishing flight-song. Crows caw along the highway. Song is the prevailing theme of the day and each source composes its melody according to its own character and performs with its own powers of instrumentation.

I am still waiting for the full liberation of the spring waters, an event full of meaning and dramatic effect which one who has not lived alone in the stillness of the northern wilderness can fully appreciate. Several times I listen for it carefully, expectantly. All is ready for it; the sun is warming, sending out steady beams of radiant heat; a current of warm air is sweeping over the land. Again I listen—and now I hear it like the roar of a distant storm approaching. Suddenly released small trickles of water turn into rushing torrents. Water pours down the ditches, rushes into the depressions in the ground in hilarious freshets and out again, down, down toward the lake. The water glitters like diamonds in the sun, fresh and beautiful, wetting, soaking the ground, dissolving the snow and the frost. I poke away a barrier in the path of the water and it rushes on in a swelling stream.

The distant thunder of Talon Chute breaks through the din and the tinkle of the freshets, weakly at first, then louder, then weaker, then louder again as the winds carrying the sound play around the rocks and the cliffs of the river gorge. At the dam the water pours over the edge in a frothy white strip, throwing into the air cascades that sparkle in the sun, and the steady solemn swish of the mighty mass flowing into the rapids comes strong and vibrant across the lake. Water is today the main theme, the foremost agent, and all nature centers upon it. Its volume, its sounds, its wonderful life-awakening humidity permeates the whole of this local world.

Last year the red-winged blackbird surprised me by returning before either the land or I expected it. What happens one year can happen also the next and I am ready for it. I listen for the familiar song, but there is no sound. I look for it, but the bird is not there. When two of them finally perch in the willows alongside the southwest marsh and announce their arrival with their first songs, *olee-o-lee-olee*, I have waited so long for them that the event is robbed of its acute joy and excitement.

The two red-wings leave no doubt about their familiarity with the place. One of them immediately proclaims his ownership of the southeast marsh and the other of the southwest reed beds. In both cases the rite of reoccupation is brief, a few mincing steps on top of the telephone post crossbar, a halfhearted puffing up of shiny black feathers, a wingspread exposing part of the scarlet epaulets, and then the song pressed forth as if by a tremendous effort. The last is of course pure pretense, a self-assertive way of showing off calculated to impress whomsoever might profit thereby. But because no one is around to take any particular notice, the song is soon ended in favor of the more urgent matter of feeding, and without further ado the two red-wings make a beeline side by side to the familiar feeding place at the house.

The flow of warmer air inspires the migrating birds with an irresistible temptation to move northward. It deposits at our feeding station a slate-colored junco that hops around looking lonesome and out of place, and a song sparrow that announces its safe homecoming with a single song. A dozen strangers of the red-wing clan volplane out of the sky and alight in the reeds, causing consternation to the two first arrived, and a display of scarlet shoulder feathers and explosions of songs greet this intrusion. A day or so later the delayed effect of this warm current of air brings on an influx of sparrows and juncos, which run head on into a cold front. This arrests any further penetration northward and the birds spread out and fill our forest with their numbers. Gray juncos pepper the melting drifts, tails aloft and wings dropped, picking eagerly the myriad edible specks that litter the ground and the snow. Their tinkling songs, like a chorus of miniature silver-toned bells assiduously shaken in dynamic musical competition, intermingle melodiously with the song sparrows' nicely articulated warbled motifs.

A flock of redpolls, their red caps well down over their brows and vivid red color splashed gaily over the striped fronts of some of them, swarms into the top of a tall poplar. The south winds have awakened the lust for travel in them too and so they have now abandoned the weed patches and the search for dried seeds among the shrubs along the lakeshore. For a few minutes the birds remain in the top of the tree, picking seeds from the poplar catkins, and their twitterings provide the neighborhood with an enchanting musical intermezzo. In a whirl of wings they dash off into the next tree for another brief snack, then into the next. But once on their way, the redpolls are not prone to linger and off they go again, dancing in bouncing flight out over the lake northward. The departing flock is almost immediately replaced by another and then still another, all yielding to the same impulse of flying north, making only brief stops here and there to restore used-up energy on their way to the land where the trees end and the barrens begin.

Two masses of air collide over the Pimisi Bay region. The warmer one is the stronger and it penetrates and spreads, pushing back the cold air. Through dense layers of ground fog torrents of rain pelt down. Big Bay and Little Bay are miraculously freed from winter's stifling harness. On the large lake, still covered with waterlogged flakes of ice, enlarging channels of free water develop in a zigzag pattern; the same steely blue shade colors both ice and water.

The sun breaks through the clouds and before a brisk south wind the ice flakes undulate with soft tinkling noises. The wind sets the creaking mass in motion, handles it roughly, and drives it up on the north shore where it accumulates frothy white like an elongated snowdrift. And with the heat of the afternoon sun upon it, the white drift drips into the lake, drop by glistening drop, and disappears.

At long last the lake is again alive and blue as the sky. Glittering wavelets curl the surface, run over it before little gusts of wind in quickly formed patches of starlight. The high water lifts logs and weirdly shaped roots and other debris out of their nests, tears them loose, and carries them down on the strong current in a sedate procession. Generous as a potentate in the distribution of its wealth, the water washes high up on the cliffs along the river and among the rocks of the lakeshore. Alder bushes and willows stand with their feet deep in the water and somewhere under their shadow a beaver gives the surface a resounding smacking with its broad fleshy tail. The rings from the impact run across the water producing abstract patterns of figures and shadings. Suddenly the spring peepers awaken and soon their bell-toned mating concert is in full force, clear and cool and insistent.

Long before its white belly alight with the long rays of the setting sun appears overhead, I hear the loon's resonant call. A second loon floating placidly in the middle of the lake answers but in quite a different tune of rhythmic and highly accentuated notes. For a few moments the two loons carry on an animated conversation and their voices reverberate handsomely back and forth between the shores. Guided by this exchange of splendid wild music the incoming loon emerges out of the blue on rapidly beating wings, swerves around High Point, sinks down on set wings, breaks the water with a swishing sound, and a minor swell froths at its breast. The loon lifts its head haughtily and I wait for the call, but the bird remains silent and relaxed. Five other loons, one after the other, surface and shake the water from their heads. All gather together in a short session of fraternal companionship, a loose group of seven streamlined great divers in their black-and-white spotted nuptial plumage. Arching its sleek body the last arrival slips under the surface, and then another, and the water closes upon the seven as if they had never been there.

The air on this first real spring evening is soft and sweet, pungent with the scents of the wet earth. The red-wings are whistling in the reeds. A winter wren, its tail flippantly erect, busily investigates dry brush heaps and rotting logs and with loud songs pouring freely from its wide-open bill announces its progress from strategic points. Farther away a hermit thrush is engaged in another type of recital, this one composed of slow and softly muted arpeggios mounting to trailing enchanted heights and delivered with consummate detachment.

Crashing in upon these harmonies, devastating the peace of the evening, someone on the other side of Little Bay bangs away with a rifle.

The return of a banded bird grows more poignant and impressive with every year that the bird reappears, simply because it is still alive. When the time comes, as inevitably it must too soon, much too soon, when I wait for it in vain, the knowledge of the details of its life imparted by the band that made the bearer into an individual separated and detached from the anonymous throng somehow mitigates the feeling of loss. The band gave it stature and importance as a fellow creature belonging to the same universal cast. And in this sense the banded bird's journey south and again northward acquires a greater measure of meaning and actuality, because the thought of this personally known mite winging its way over such great and hostile distances, practically alone and sometimes for the first time in its life, can now make me better realize the immensity of this annual avian undertaking and the proportions of its risks.

Ethereality, is not this the migratory bird's chief character and attribute? Here today, gone tomorrow, borne upon air, directed by an instantaneous and inordinately keen sensitivity to the shifting environmental situation that bids it prepare for and then start the long journey; the urge created by subtle physiological changes supplying energy and motivation for an effort that seems out of all proportion to a creature as fragile as a bird! This, we know, is part of the combination of inducements that produces within the bird the emotional state necessary to impel it to set out. We know that some birds for a short time before the start consume food beyond their ordinary requirements in order to store a reserve of expendable energy in the form of fat to take with them on the way. We have seen the restlessness that often precedes the actual take-off, suggesting the strong reluctance of the bird to sever the bond with the familiar scene and indicating the force of the impulse that breaks this bond with the land and casts the bird out into the night upon the initial stage of its stupendous enterprise. Despite the headway researchers have recently made with the aid of modern contrivances such as radar, the bird's capacity of orientation over thousands of miles and its return to precisely the same tiny dot on the map where it spent its first nesting season, in not a few instances also where it hatched, is still a largely unsolved problem. By what magic does the bird achieve such accurate navigation? May it not be that we, having eaten too greedily of the fruits of the tree of knowledge, have so dulled our innate senses that we can no longer either imagine or understand the essence of the simple inborn sense of orientation which necessity once developed in primitive man? The birds must possess this sense in an exceptionally high degree to achieve their migratory feat. Among men only the specially trained and experienced woodsman may still retain some of it. Ask him by what means he finds his bearings and he will tell you that he just knows one direction from another in the same way as we automatically know how to walk. And as the ability to walk requires the action of many nerves and muscles, so also does the bird's ability to find its way require the cooperation of many senses, the exact workings of each of which are natural and perhaps quite simple once they are known. Undoubtedly the most important among them are an accurate memory for landmarks, a sharp sensitivity to what goes on in the environment, and a capacity to detect and to compensate for directional errors with which the forces of nature sometimes confound the aerial traveler.

Good luck—how much of this commodity does the bird need to bring it safely back to its breeding grounds? What is the exact figure of the bird's migratory mortality? Surely the need for luck is very great—the chance of making a successful dash for cover as the predator attacks, the luck of good weather, of finding food at the right time and in the right place, of being on the lucky side of the fractional difference that separates safety from disaster. Across distances of thousands of miles beset with narrow escapes the bird returns, ready and eager to throw itself into yet another game of hide-and-seek with life and death, of risk-filled hairbreadth escapes, with the same total abandon that characterizes all its activities in the fulfillment of its natural functions and its destiny. Surely this is the meaning of life, this irreverent teetering atop the crest of eventualities that seems to be the essence of the bird's life, without premeditation, without fear! Surely this is freedom in its purest sense!

The reappearance of the white-throated sparrow known as Blue-green was a complete surprise. This was the fourth time she had returned from migration since she was banded, but for some reason I had missed seeing her the previous year and consequently wrote her off the record as presumed dead. But there she was on this beautiful morning in May very much alive, hopping gaily over the rock wall and under the trap, ever on the *qui vive* and ravenously hungry. To make doubly sure of her identity I got the resurrected ghost into my hand and read her band.

From the first day I knew her, Blue-green proclaimed herself a female by her short wings, and later on her behavior confirmed this. As the custom is among the white-throats, she built the nest herself and incubated the eggs without help from her mate. But if she had not had the good luck to make the long trip south and back so many times as she did, the matter of territorial faithfulness in the white-throated female would have remained unknown and unproven to me. As it was she granted me three seasons in which to observe her movements and habits.

From at least two viewpoints the matter of territorial fidelity or the lack of it in the female is important. First, having the responsibility of building the nest, she also selects the site. It must be in a suitable and comparatively safe place, usually in a nice sheltered depression in the ground, sometimes low in a bush. White-throated sparrows are known to have two broods in a season, and the second nest site is often chosen at a distance from the first one and nearly always in a safer place with better cover. Second nests have also as a rule a higher rate of success. There is of course a wider selection of nest sites available in a larger area than in a constricted one, and therefore to make a good choice it is important for the female not to be hemmed in by territorial borders. Blue-green had no respect for her mate's territorial limits and if she saw fit to build her second nest several hundred feet from the first one, and outside his established domain to boot, she did so without asking anybody's permission. Secondly, for a female widowed in the midst of the breeding season the chances of remating sometimes depend on her mobility. When this happened to Blue-green during her second nesting season she demonstrated her complete independence of any established borders by getting herself engaged to a male at High Point and placing her second nest for the season over a thousand feet from the one she had used in the nesting with her deceased partner.

During the span of her short life and in the course of her lucky returns Blue-green obliged me with by revealing another interesting fact of which I was unaware. The stripes that adorned her crown were ill-defined and mottled brown in color, not conspicuously black and white as in some of the white-throats. She also had a dusky grayish throat patch, not the flashy pure-white one with which the white-throated sparrow is usually depicted and from which it acquires its name. When Blue-green lay in my hand for the last time her crown was as mottled brownish and her bib as dusky gray as they had been when she came into my trap four years earlier. Obviously her coloration did not alter with age; nor did it have anything to do with sex, for in the course of time I found many singing males in the same plumage as Blue-green. How normal the bright color patterns of the white-throated sparrow are is indicated by the fact that of all the white-throats I have on record slightly over half belong to Blue-green's color phase.

The chill of the day in late April and the bird's arriving famished from the nightly flight combined to bring the myrtle warbler down from the tops of the trees in the early morning to pick and eat of the suet at our table. Although myrtle warblers nest regularly every year in the evergreens surrounding the house, this had never happened before. I was surprised that this kind of food appealed to so specialized and largely insectivorous a little gourmet as this warbler. But it appears that the taste and nutritional properties of suet are close enough to the accustomed diet of most insectivorous birds to be accepted as a substitute in an emergency.

Exquisite in his fancy spring feathers, the appearance of the myrtle warbler on the feeder was like the sight of the sun breaking through the clouds from a dull sky. His contrasting black and white markings against the subdued bluish-gray groundtone of his plumage enhanced a hundredfold the brilliant lemon-yellow spots that adorned his crown, wings, and rump. The bird looked like a butterfly of exotic origin. Moving cautiously at first, he soon fell to feeding ravenously and for a time the appeasement of his hunger overruled all other impulses. He did not watch where he was going. . . . And the trap sprang shut upon a vastly bewildered bird. The next moment he was on his back in my open hand with a bright red circlet around his right leg and free to go.

Red settled upon the land centered around our house and made it into his three-dimensional territory, and today he returned to it for the third time in faithful and exact obedience to the proclivities laid down within him. From Cuba or Central America or the southern United States—how do I know?—over more than a thousand miles he came back once again to this tiny familiar speck on the map to mate and to nest. In the course of the years of our acquaintance he always showed up among the first migrants of his own species, most often the first one. I hardly had to make sure that the bird who dropped the first myrtle-warbler theme upon the air, *zree-zree-zree-zree*, was actually Red or that the first glimpse I caught of something black, white, and yellow was connected with a red band. Memory and habit played their momentous and elemental roles in bringing about his unfailing return to the nesting territory he had acquired in the first spring of his life.

Early in the season, while he still had the place to himself, Red ranged over a far larger area than he was to possess eventually. He held it magically by his presence and his singing. But with the arrival of other myrtle warblers his domain underwent a shrinking process. The extent to which his boundaries were affected depended on the number of myrtle warbler males settling on adjoining premises and on the amount of efficient supervision of which he was capable, especially under pressure. In fact, the borders of his land had the quality of an accordion, being not too difficult to push in or out according the environmental influences he was apt to respond to most intensely at any given moment.

Naturally Red allowed no encroachments without energetic opposition. He expressed his feelings chiefly by song and threatening attitudes, spread tail and wings let down. Comparatively rarely he became involved in real fighting, breast to breast and bill to bill, and the two adversaries caught in so fierce a battle that they dropped to the ground like leaves falling in the autumn. Success or defeat, territorial enlargement or shrinkage, ultimately hinged upon such things as individual prowess and inclination, on the speed of reactions and the distance each found himself from the center of his normal activities. This marvelously appropriate interaction between circumstances and events, between creatures and environment, efficiently protects the natural balance, and concurrence with it is always the better part of valor.

Along the lakeshore a small flock of male myrtle warblers alight in the trees and after a brief rest meander on, feeding as they go. Among them is one female, distinguishable from the males by her dress, discreetly brownish in color but lacking none of the dazzling yellow spots characteristic of the species. Quite innocently the group transgresses the boundaries of Red's domain. Ever on the alert against intrusions, innocent or not, Red greets them in a state of high excitement. He throws back his head, exposing his beautiful white throat patch, and with his bill wide open and pointing skyward he treats the trespassers to several loud songs, his most impressive expression of challenge and protest. For good measure he chases any who come within chasing distance, dashing hither and yon after the intruders.

Suddenly he catches sight of the female. His reaction is intense; he utters small chittering notes and dashes after her in a series of lightning pursuits, she first, he close behind her. She ends up perched on a twig in the midst of Red's territory and looks around. She does not avoid him, she does not oppose him, and by the way she moves even I can plainly see that she is going to stay. Red dashes at her again—but suddenly brakes his speed, veers, stops, never gets close to her, lets her sit where she is. Is it her looks that all of a sudden persuade him she is different from the trespassing males, or is it her behavior? Or is it a combination of both that so abruptly transforms his aggressive comportment into one of tolerance and nonresistance, that makes it possible for him to accept the presence of the inevitable companion, the rightful shareholder of all that is his?

CHAPTER EIGHT

"Halfway Houses on the Road to Heaven"

The phoebe pair are sitting on their lookout post, a bare branchlet that sticks out into the open from the top of a dead aspen. The birds sit very close together. Obviously the barrier of individual distance has broken down between them. Not very far away, quite within sight, their finished nest is tucked away in the shadow of the eaves of our house on a little shelf Len put up for them. The nest contains one egg.

Eight days ago, after three of their first set of five eggs in another nest were stolen, one pierced I do not know by whom, and the fifth left untouched, the phoebes began the construction of this nest. Like the first one, it is artfully shaped of mud and green moss. Now the color of the fresh moss is fading and the mud is drying. The walls of the cup are molded into the precise form of the female's breast and belly, with the egg resting in the middle. The female's instinct in creating the masterpiece is independently her own and in this case faultless.

At first the phoebe worked at her construction with great

dispatch and eagerness, but toward the end her pace slackened considerably. Finally, with curiously slowed-down movements like those in a moving picture being run at half speed, she carefully inserted the last fine fiber into the nest lining. During the current season, unless misfortune should interrupt this nesting also, a revival of the need for this particular task will hardly arise again.

So with the new nest all ready the pair allow themselves two days' holiday before the female is ready to lay the first egg. They go abroad together and I often find them nonchalantly flipping their tails in places where the sun shines brightly and the catch of flying insects is good. At this time their concern about the nest is at a low ebb, for there is nothing in it. Only at dawn before the sun rises and at night after sunset the male is back on the lookout post in the aspen, engaged in giving his

regular dawn and sunset recitals. This is his way of declaring the attachment that nonetheless exist between him and her and the empty nest.

But now with the first egg in the nest the situation is entirely different. The holiday is over. Both birds keep a much closer watch over the nest, seldom getting out of sight of it. When one is not there, the other one usually is. The cooperation between them is more intimate; they are closer to each other and closer to the common object of shared responsibility, the nest.

From the lookout post the male suddenly flings himself into the air and abandons himself to a wonderful flight-song. The song is composed of a loud whistled note followed by a string of *phoe-be* notes in quick succession. The delicious strain ended, he alights beside his mate, but whether or not his performance moved her in any way, she gives no sign.

Every so often the two birds make graceful sallies into the air to catch flies on the wing. Here is one for him, there is another for her. They never miss. Once or twice the female ends up in the red-cherry tree that stands decked in a profusion of white blossoms. She looks lovely in the scented surroundings. She flips her tail as she gazes at the nest from this closer distance. Quite innocently a chickadee comes within range of what the phoebe deems her private zone. Peremptorily she chases the chickadee, and later she does the same to a buzzing hummingbird and a trespassing Blackburnian warbler. During each chase she announces the nonadmittance ruling by a terse double note, pronounced by me *sit-up—sit-up*.

That night when the sun has disappeared and the dusk lingers and deepens in the soft spring evening the male pounces upon the female and in one swoop bears her to the ground in conjugal union. This is accompanied by a loud outburst of twittering notes. He repeats the performance once again. None the worse, the female shakes herself and preens her feathers lightly while the male wipes his bill thoroughly on the twig upon which he is sitting, all in the name of relieved tension. By this time it is almost dark and I can only with difficulty see the birds as they move. Quietly the female slips into the nest on the shelf and the male disappears for the night among the branches midway up the spire of a balsam fir. All is still. The next morning the female remains in the nest until an hour after sunrise, while the male perches on top of our open window with his face turned to the nest. She begins to fidget a little, looks around. And when she leaves a minute or two later, a second egg lies gleaming white beside the first one.

Two places, one on the southeastern slope and the other on the plateau behind the house, are brighter and lighter than the rest of the forest. Here the broad-leaved trees outnumber the evergreens and their growth is not so dense. Light filters through between them more generously than elsewhere and encourages a greater variety of shrubs and smaller ground cover such as sedges and grasses, bedstraw and asters and many other flowering plants. Here and there patches of bracken grow thick as a forest of green umbrellas, shielding the earth from the direct sun. Both places are dry, but each one possesses a luxuriant source of water, the overflow from the spring on the southeastern slope and a woodland pool hiding under a small clump of evergreens at the edge of the plateau. Because of their similarity in features and vegetation, these two places naturally appeal to birds with the same habitat requirements. And this is how it came about that identical groups of birds, each group consisting of a pair of chestnut-sided warblers, a pair of redstarts, and a pair of mourning warblers, took up residence in each of the two places.

To achieve a nonaggressive type of coexistence among the three pairs in each area without too great interference from the others, certain measures of accommodation are required so that each of them has a fair chance of benefiting from what the surroundings have to offer of food and opportunities. Differences in appearance and behavior contribute to this end, whereby each species, closely related though all three are, finds its place in a loosely indicated niche that suits the bird's particular habits and supplies its wants to greatest advantage, and the temptation and need for any one species to encroach upon the franchise of the others is thus largely avoided.

The speckled beauty of the chestnut-sided warbler, with its streaks and wing-bars, the chestnut-colored line along its flanks, its design of black and white, the olive-green-tinted edgings of the feathers on the back, shoulders, and wings, and the lemon-yellow crown patch, admirably fits into the surroundings halfway up the trees where dappled sunshine and varying shades of green leaves predominate. The same cannot be said of the satiny black plumage with orange flashes on wings and tail that adorns the male redstart. But the fact that this vivacious bird with intensity and dash is always on the move, wings and tail widely fanned, somehow camouflages the conspicuousness of its dress and lends it an air of useful disguise, for strange as it seems black is a shade of cryptical value against the sylvan background. The mourning warbler's plumage, shading gradually from olive-green above to bright yellow below, with no striking markings except a bluish hood and a throat patch of mottled black that looks like crape, blends nicely with the shaded lighting under the bracken where the bird spends much of its time as well as with the sunlit foliage higher up in the trees. The name given the bird by no means refers to any subdued behavior associated with grief. Of this the mourning warbler does not exhibit a trace; only its song, flat in key, slightly mournful in quality, is in keeping with the patch on the throat, not its gay and winsome ways.

The territories of the birds are superimposed upon one another. On the slope the space is a little larger than on the plateau and offers slight extensions of respective borders in various directions beyond those of the neighbor. At first the relations between the three species are astonishingly compatible; each resists only the intrusion of its own kind. During such resistance their singing comes to its fullest and most meaningful employment, but the musicality of their song themes, which so enchants the human listener, is of far less importance than the self-assertive and aggressive implications of the song. It expresses drive and nervous tension, and its tonal beauty is but a product of chance.

Of the three birds, the chestnut-sided warbler likes best to enact his open-mouthed singing from the higher places, the upper branches of young trees, the top branches of the shrubs, whence he can more easily keep an eye on what goes on about him. Like his movements, his singing is fast and lively. Pronouncing each strophe with great emphasis, he often crams no less than twenty songs into the fleeting minute. He leaves neither neighbors nor trespassers long in doubt of his whereabouts nor does he neglect to inform them through which points his territorial borders are considered to be drawn. As to the redstart, it seems incongruous for so ethereal a creature to advertise himself with so abrupt and terse a song, though in combination his song and looks could hardly serve the redstart's bent toward ostentation better. Unlike the two others, the mourning warbler much prefers the lower heights of the forest strata. The tempo of his singing, as of his movements, is deliberate and smooth; six or seven low-pitched songs are all he can crowd into a minute and he always accompanies his singing by softly batting his wings against his golden flanks.

At this early stage of the breeding season, migrants passing through the territories of the six warblers produce the crowning excitement of the day. The birds react quickly to the invasion; the chestnut-sided warblers tilt their tails at a jauntier angle and drop their wingtips lower, the redstarts flash their wings and tails, and the mourning warblers flit hither and yon batting their wings against their sides. The more excited they are, the more exaggerated become their movements and their displays. Whenever the situation demands additional emphasis song underlines the posturing, the challenging and exhibitionist movements.

The first female to enter upon these scenes is a mourning

warbler on the plateau. She takes no notice whatever of the male, although I am sure she is not blind. But the instant he catches sight of her he undergoes a drastic change in behavior and attitude. He begins to court her, hopping from twig to twig, he follows her as she moves around feeding, preening, and feeding again. She leads him a merry dance. She flies down to the lake, drinks, bathes lightly in a little pool, throwing the water over head and shoulders, splashing with her wings, ducking, and the water runs off her pretty feathers like drops of mercury. She flies off and the male dashes after her. As he catches up with her he resumes his hopping from twig to twig and the batting of his wings softly against his sides.

The arrival of the females causes some changes in the behavior of the males. They react much more vigorously especially to intruders than they did before. Even fellow territory-holders, should they perchance approach too closely a neighbor's female or the spot she eventually designates as the nest site, can no longer claim almost total immunity from persecution as once they did. The release of the males' aggressive impulses is triggerlike and explosive. Their hostilities take different forms—duet singing, squealing, the stealthy stalking of the trespasser, more rarely straight fighting breast to breast falling-leaf fashion, claw catching claw. The distance from bird to bird or from a bird to any of its vital territorial points acquires increasing significance and in a crisis often decides the outcome of the contention.

Surveying his domain from his singing post, the chestnut-sided warbler suddenly discovers a strange male of his own kind and dashes at the intruder. The violence of his attack promptly unseats the trespasser and, taking possession of the perch the latter just vacated, the resident gives a loud song. Relaxation of tension, self-assertion, and appeasement are all mixed in the warbler's triumphal outburst. But the opponent is not so easily discouraged. He espies the female and approaches her tentatively. This precipitates a prolonged session of chasing between the two males. In abrupt turns and giddy swoops the chase goes in and out of bushes and trees, down among the not yet fully unfurled bracken, up into the trees again. Almost, but never quite, catching up with the intruder, the resident warbler lets out piercing squeals. The noise and the dashing about greatly excite the female. She cannot contain herself; she plunges into the fray but withdraws the next moment as if the fight were not really her business. And the wild chase goes on. Occasionally the resident bird stops and gives vent to another loud triumphal song. Occasionally the trespasser tries to do likewise, but since he has no territorial rights to justify his would-be effusion, his effort fails as the other renews the charge.

The greater the commotion caused by the two antagonists and the longer the disturbance lasts, the more widespread are its effects. Excitement is highly contagious and soon engulfs every bird within sight and earshot. A neighboring myrtle warbler gets in the way of the chase, shivers its wings, and says *tock* several times. A pair of magnolia warblers flit nervously around the combatants and explode into loud scolding. The resident mourning warbler, happening upon the scene by mere chance, sings one song and flees. A red-eyed vireo *miews* its disapproval of the peace disturbers and thereby distracts the chestnut-sided warbler from the chase; unexpectedly he turns upon the vireo and runs it out of the territory. A melee ensues, with an assembly of birds flitting about squealing, chipping, and flapping their wings. The turmoil affects the drive of the strange chestnut-sided warbler, the cause of it all, and he steals away quietly while the others continue the commotion. But a few minutes pass before the sudden removal of the disturbing presence penetrates the cognizance of all concerned and emotions are subdued.

Long before the females begin to take any notice of their respective mates' courting overtures, they tour the territories investigating nest sites. Quite matter-of-factly they search for the particular place that appeals to them. The chestnut-sided is attracted by raspberry canes leaning together to form a crotch, or small bushes or even a bracken after its green fronds are fully unfolded—any small crotch well hidden not more than about two feet above the ground. The redstart prefers young trees or tall bushes, but larger trees will also do at times, provided they have some kind of platform to which she can securely attach her compact nest at a height of about five to twenty feet. The mourning warbler hides her nest on the ground, tucks it away into a recess suited for the purpose. And after the building is completed, every time she goes to the nest she carefully preserves the secret of its whereabouts by elaborating a labyrinthine approach down deep through the undercover, starting very far from the actual site.

The female redstart on the plateau, demure in her olive-brown and white plumage with pale yellow flashes on wings and tail, finds two crotches in a soft maple six feet from the ground. Both appeal to her and she hops from one to the other, sits in them, nudges her breast deep down into their depths. They fit nicely. She begins to carry nesting materials, fine tendrils and grasses, strips of thin birch bark, hairs dropped by the snowshoe hare. She places some of it in each crotch. Obviously the two sites are so close together, less than two feet apart, that she is unable to separate them; to her they are as one. Soon she has built a neat platform in each.

Her mate is a young redstart no more than a year old; not yet having attained the full adult plumage, he looks like the female except for a few black spots indicating his coming of age. He sings continuously, short abrupt songs. He gives his mate no assistance in her growing confusion about the two nests. But every so often he involves himself in fights with trespassers, one with a yellow warbler who loses to the redstart a beautiful yellow feather that drops twirling to the ground.

Presently the redstart female finds a piece of white tissue paper that looks like white birch bark. She carries it into the north nest. No sooner has she placed it there than she tears it out again, and with it most of the half-finished nest. Violently ejected tendrils, fine grasses, bits of birch bark, soft and pliant as satin, attach themselves to various twigs on their way to the ground and hang there. The bird carries the tissue away and as this, too, hooks on to a twig, she begins to tear it into small pieces. But soon she tires, drops the whole thing, and goes off to feed.

Upon her return she sees only one nest, in the south crotch, almost completed. Her perplexities vanish with the convenient, more or less accidental tearing out of the north nest. A nest is a nest and one is quite enough to maintain her adequate response and to promote its future important function. If once there were two nests and she saw only one nest at a time, and if she actually were confused about the exact position of each because she saw double, now this confused viewpoint related to the north and the south crotches in the maple is a stage of the past. She plucks from their hangers the materials torn from the north crotch, also the white tissue that looks like birch bark, which she dropped. Adeptly she weaves all of this into the south nest, carefully smooths the edge of the cup with her chin. The nest grows in size, beautifully molded in form, lined with fine hairs and plant down, adequately camouflaged. With the interwoven pieces of birch bark and white tissue paper it looks like a spot of dappled sunshine, just air, no body. It is a masterpiece. But it is never to hold a speckled redstart egg, because a few days later, for reasons of their own, the pair move to the other end of the territory. Who can follow the precise ways in which circumstances play upon the strings of nature's creatures?

The redstart on the southeastern slope has her nest already finished when I discover it stuck into the crotch of a sapling birch. There is nothing remarkable about the site, but the nest is built with an unusually thick bottom. Three days later, unlike the pea in the Hans Christian Andersen's story, the first egg lies on top of the princess's seven mattresses. In another three days the female sits daintily upon her pedestal, warming three eggs.

When I look in upon her again two days later, she is off the nest hopping about and chipping in great excitement. This she never did before at my approach. What's wrong? The nest is empty. She keeps treating me as an enemy, hops around and scolds me roundly. Who took the eggs? And while my curiosity may indeed endanger her and the nest, because inadvertently I may leave signs that others with more predacious intentions may follow, I am utterly puzzled by her behavior and the whole situation.

Nor do I know why I return two days later or what I expect to find except the place deserted. What I do find to my amazement is the bird feeding peacefully and calmly near the nest. This time she does not treat me as a predator. Moreover, the nest is another story higher and contains—I can hardly believe my eyes—two new speckled eggs. What she achieved in those two days is a feat. In less than thirty-six hours she managed to build half a new nest on top of the old one, and therein she laid two eggs that could hardly have been dropped less than twenty-four hours apart on the newly constructed bale. In another day she is sitting on top of her two-story building incubating four eggs. And as I appear to check on her and again disappear, she only turns her head slightly.

The eggs hatch in due time. On this day the redstart remains sitting upon her sprawling almost naked mites with complete confidence until my hand nearly touches her. But then, with an elegant little swoop, off she goes. She drops to the ground and in a trice her whole attitude changes. My eyes fasten upon her fascinated. With curved wings, their tips trailing, and her lemon-yellow markings flashing brightly in the shade under the trees, she runs along the ground, hops on to a moss-covered log. There she crouches facing me, her whole body held in a horizontal line, her curved wings bulging from her sides and shivering. In this pose she slowly pivots from side to side, as an electric fan pivots back and forth upon its stand.

Hastily I adjust the green leaf over the nest before I slowly move away, obeying an impulse to relieve the tension of the bird on the log. The slow-motion gyrating from side to side of the little figure is so entrancing that I cannot take my eyes off her. Its hypnotic effect is real. The inducement to move away from the nest and to be attracted instead to the bird on the log is rendered not only plausible but compelling by her play acting. This is an exciting discovery. The redstart's display, I may now affirm from my own experience, is not just a form of behavior whose meaning we assume, it actually has a mesmerizing-effect upon the beholder, the potential natural marauder not to be excluded, that distracts the attention from the nest and focuses it on the bird on the log.

Nine days later the young redstarts leave their nest safely. At last I can satisfy my curiosity about the fate of the first three eggs. I find them embedded half decayed in the company of several fat maggots in the ample bottom of the lower section of the two-story nest.

It is tempting to speculate upon what happened to make the redstart bury her first set of eggs. Birds, notably the yellow warbler, are known to bury their eggs in this way after a cowbird's egg has been intruded among them. What induced the redstart to interrupt activities commanded by so strong a drive as the parental? The impulse must have been compelling, yet not strong enough to make her abandon the site. Perhaps, unbeknown to me, a fourth egg had been added to the first three and then stolen or destroyed by some untraced predator. The shock of such an event may well have been sufficient to make her look upon the remaining three eggs as foreign objects, things that did not belong to her and were best put out of sight. So she simply built another nest on top of them.

Red, the chipping sparrow with the red band on the left leg, is not like the others of his species. He sings a different tune. As a medium of communication, the song is, of course, of great significance to the songbirds. Given so limited a scope of vocali-

zation, the composition of the song and the ease with which it may be recognized are also of importance, especially in the case of such simple phrasing as that of the chipping sparrow, one continuous trill on the same pitch lasting about two seconds.

Red's song is unusual in that it is composed of two parts, two separate trills, sometimes of even three complete trills. Curiously, his songs are shorter than the common one of the chipping sparrow, because the trills are shorter, lasting altogether only one second. Red makes up for this abbreviation by repeating his songs more often, eight to nine times instead of six times a minute, which is the rate at which the ordinary chipping sparrow usually sings. I can easily make this comparison, because Red and his common-song neighbor do not live far apart and they often sing at the same time. The season for song is auspicious, for the birds are still alone and just now preoccupied with establishing the outlines of their territories before the arrival of the females.

It is interesting that birds hear and interpret sounds of much greater variety than they are able to utter themselves. Though Red's song is out of the ordinary, the other chipping sparrow and I have no difficulty in recognizing it as that of a chipping sparrow. I have not studied birdsong extensively enough to be able to explain precisely the relationship between the variations in their vocalizations and the birds' receptory capacity. But from the way in which some songbirds express themselves it is easy to realize that their songs may have a wide margin of variability without this hampering those who are within earshot and in some way profit by the knowledge and their ability to identify the singer.

A few days later a marked decline in Red's singing is to be noted and I know from experience that this signals a change in the situation out there under the pines. With the center of his territory right on my doorstep and the bird under my eyes most of the time, fear for his untimely demise, suggested by his sudden silence, is quicky and happily eliminated. I am therefore not surprised to find him closely associating with a nice little partner whose red cap and white eyebrow line are slightly less pronounced in color and delineation than Red's own. She wears a blue band on her right leg and thereby identifies herself as Red's mate of last year when both of them occupied the same territory.

This is a happy coincidence, for I would not say that this meeting results from personal faithfulness on the part of either. I have already pointed out that a curious combination of memory and expert orientation is responsible for landing the returned bird with remarkable precision at or near the place whence it departed the previous autumn on its journey south. Faithfulness to the locality is a powerful agent in the lives of

[159]

many birds. It assures good homing ability when this is required. Quite often it also substitutes for the need of long-range personal fidelity. In some species of birds personal fidelity from year to year may not be a profitable quality to develop, lest it become too strong and thus prevent another attachment upon the loss of a first mate.

In the case of Red and Blue the land is the matchmaker that brings them together for the second time. The rituals of sex recognition, of getting used to the presence of each other, of personal recognition, which are necessary for an adequate measure of cooperation, have to be performed all over again to the same full extent as the first time they met and lived together a year ago. Besides, the time involved in the courtship is a valuable and subtle activator that through one event after another gradually brings about the concurrence of the birds' emotional interdependence. No shortcuts actually are possible. The only advantage gained from this being the birds' second honeymoon is perhaps a smoother temperamental synchronization. Or at least so it seems to me.

At the completion of these ceremonies the togetherness of the two birds is almost absolute. They feed together, sit together, fly together, she leading the way and he escorting her. They separate only when such essentially male activities as advertising or defending the territory demand his prompt attention, or when particularly female preoccupations, such as nest-building, absorb her.

Blue soon decides upon a site for her nest in a tuft of needles rather high up in a white pine. The leaves of the white pine are well adapted to serve her as a good nest base; they are shorter and softer and there are five of them in the cluster instead of two as in the red pine. She has, however, no objection to red pines. Last year she built her nest in the one next to the white pine. What she primarily looks for is good cover, a bushy spot, and some kind of seat to which she can attach her nest securely. And here in the north she finds this combination most often in the evergreens, small and tall.

She goes about her nest-building quite on her own, with or without Red in attendance. She flies a long way from the nest tree to collect her materials, a type of strong and pliant fine black rootlets. She tugs at them, twisting and turning. Whoops! Their sudden release upsets her balance. She picks them up and it is amazing what a number of them she is able to cram crosswise into her small dainty bill. She espies another good piece. She promptly drops her collection, tears the piece loose, forgets the heap she dropped and hops away in search of more. Finally she carries a load to the nest. She puts it in the chosen spot, intertwines the pieces, scratches with her feet and presses her breast among them, and all this is accomplished with her whole body strongly vibrating. She picks loose pieces from the outside and folds them over the edge, tucks them in, this also with strong trembling motions of her whole body. Her pace of work slackens during the afternoon, but in the evening the structure presents a dense spot in the middle of the tuft of white pine needles.

During the night it begins to rain and the weather turns cold and miserable, the beginning of an interval of several cold and windy days. Gradually the need and the search for food to combat the chilliness engage all her energies. For a day or two her preoccupation with the nest dwindles because she has not yet acquired a very strong feeling about it. It has nothing alive in it yet. Only once in a while when she happens to pass by she sees it and goes to sit down by it or in it. At that moment the sight of the nest exercises upon her a compelling influence, but apart from that, out of sight, out of memory, and the urge to feed prevails.

As the work on the nest progresses and the time for the egg laying approaches, Red's excitement at the sight of her increases to a high pitch. During this stage of their courtship Red's chief aid is persuasion. The intensity of his excitement is always neatly balanced against Blue's resistance. He pounces upon her, but she escapes and only after a wild pursuit is he able to bring her to earth where their bodies unite amid a great flutter of wings and loud cheepings. She escapes quickly, shivering her wings, shakes herself, and hops away with her wings still trembling as if the residue of her emotion is too strong to be appeased immediately.

Gradually the gravitational point of their emotional balance shifts. As the egg laying is being completed Red now simply catches her when the opportune moment presents itself. And she surrenders, often with her bill full of food, then blithely enjoys her slightly delayed meal. She performs these rites quite demurely until the mood leaves her entirely. Thereafter she plays the evasive game lightly, inoffensively. The effect upon Red is to the point. Gradually his excitement subsides and he returns once more to his previous occupations, his travels around the territory, his singing, and his feeding, while Blue sits on the nest warming the eggs. This is a period of well-earned rest for both of them.

After the eggs hatch Red's interest in the family rises considerably, until he shares almost equally with the female the labors connected with the nest and the young. Occasionally he even sits down to warm the brood, sometimes taking over from Blue directly by a shift, a she-off-he-on routine. Soon the nestlings need brooding no longer. And so during a season of indefatigable labors Red and Blue eventually present the world with a progeny of seven safely fledged chipping sparrows from their two nests.

When Blue disappears in the early fall she is gone forever. But Red returns and survives three more years. Although he faithfully comes back to his old territory in our dooryard each spring and always takes up residence there first, his nesting locality is moved to a place a few hundred feet to the south. The influence of the female, Red's new mate in this case, has to to be reckoned with in most situations.

So far as I can judge, the juncos' choice of nest site is a dangerous one because it lacks a backdoor escape hatch. In a most picturesque situation, it is tucked into a recess under a gray rock surrounded by soft green mosses. The juncos have to duck under its low opening to get into the nest chamber. The female who fashioned the nest bed in this tiny grotto obviously relies for its safety solely upon its concealment. And indeed, despite the number of things that prowl and crawl and sneak around in the forest by day and by night, in seven out of ten cases, broadly speaking, her confidence is justified.

Inside the nest, like small dark fluffballs, two junco nestlings repose, their recently opened eyes shining like stars in the half light. Within the next two days they will be ready to leave. Nearby, alarmed by my inopportune presence, the parents utter their abrupt smacking warning notes, for the benefit of the young as much as for me. A collection of green caterpillars dangling from their bills shakes violently at each utterance. The male takes the intrusion with far less equanamity than does the female. He flips his wings nervously and swallows the caterpillars; after that he smacks better. The female neither flips her wings nor swallows her caterpillars. She is obviously quite impervious to her well-hidden nest's being in danger and she only signals to the young not to betray themselves. And indeed they do not. By her behavior, which confuses more than it reveals, I would never have known where the nest was had I not happened to discover it before I saw her.

Early the next morning the nest is empty. I hear the male singing, an occupation he has all but given up with the nestlings' increasing demands upon his food-bringing energies. He sings—and in no plainer language could he tell me the sad story of the little female's having been taken, together with her young ones, from their secret abode that very night. I never knew the identity of the predator that stumbled upon the junco grotto, nor what led its steps in so profitable a direction. Perhaps only the whiff of scent carried in double dose, as so often it is upon the nightly dew, steered the stalking prowler.

The male continues to sing for several days. Then he is silent.

I read the code and duly record the information—he has found a new partner. After that the detailed sequence of the junco events escapes me, for my attention is devoted to other things.

One day I put my foot down unknowingly almost right on the new junco nest. It is ingeniously recessed into a mosaic carpet of green Shreber's moss and gray reindeer moss and over the doorway a curtain of fine green grasses hangs down from a small tussock. Four young juncos explode under my feet from this beautiful haven. They scatter in the surrounding cover. Startled, I remain motionless. A baby moves, cheeps. Instantly the female dashes at me. Landing on the ground with her wings wide open and her tail with its flashing white outer feathers spread like a fan, she creeps and wriggles in front of me. Uncertain how to extricate myself safely without trampling a baby to death, I am glad to take her hint. Gingerly I follow in her wake, setting my feet down very carefully, until she leads me out of the danger zone. The smacking notes of the parents pursue me, but from the fledglings among the blueberry wisps there is not a sound, not a move.

About three weeks later, the young juncos emerge from their hiding in the natal surroundings onto the arena of the feeding station. In their brownish lightly striped juvenile plumage they look more like ordinary sparrows than slate-colored juncos. When one of the parents appears they run up, crouch, and beg, but get very little in exchange for their fluttering wings and vocal supplications. A few days later they are altogether out of their babyhood and graduated into the class of independent individuals.

It so happens that at this time several of the birds which ordinarily feed on the ground suddenly raise their food-finding sights to the feeders suspended from wires five or six feet from the ground. This came about probably from the ovenbird's seeing the nuthatch feeding from the high feeder and then trying it himself. And when the younger-generation white-throated sparrows saw the ovenbird having a feast, they too flew up and had a feast. But the young junco outstrips all of them by performing an act of straight imitation. It flies up on to the wire roof of an aerial trip-trapping cage which hangs from the wire and is set not for trapping but for feeding. There the junco stands craning its neck and with one eye observes how a chickadee alights below him on a perch fixed to facilitate entrance into the feeder, thence hops into the cage, picks a piece of peanut, and flies out. The next instant the junco repeats the chickadee's performance exactly, step by step, and the successive movements of a figure skater, doing a school figure, could not have been more precisely executed.

In this connection I cannot resist the temptation to insert a few more examples of interesting spontaneous acts performed by my birds. A chickadee alights on top of the wire mesh with which I have covered a drip-trap pail of water to prevent accidental drowning. It tries to drink but cannot reach the water through the mesh. Slightly frustrated and also a bit curious, the chickadee picks at a leaf suspended from the wire with its stem in the water. The leaf is loose and the chickadee pulls it out. A drop of water adheres to the end of the stem. The chickadee sees the drop, recognizes it as water, and drinks. It is familiar with drops—even those suspended from icicles, to the slippery surface of which in the winter the bird often clings with the agility of an acrobat to drink. To pull out the leaf and drink from the end of its stem, while it cannot be interpreted as a premeditated act, is nonetheless a sensitive creature's logical reaction to a series of accidental events from which, on the basis of previous experience, it draws the best possible profit.

A more uncommon measure of adaptability is perhaps involved in the behavior of a gray jay. The gray jay is one of my favorite birds. It has a lovely plushy way of moving, a bright curiosity in its brown eyes, and it commands a wide variety of soft notes with which it advertises its whereabouts and its moods. Belonging to the reputedly intelligent crow family, it may be expected to show better sense than most birds, although the degree of intelligence is more often to be attributed to the individual than to the species or family as a whole. I am feeding the gray jay, throwing courtesy balls on the ground for it to pick up. The jay hops around giving its soft alert notes and collects a load of balls. It sees another piece. But usually when birds, including blue jays, try to pick up more than they can manage, they drop their original load and forget all about it. Not so my gray jay. Carefully it lays aside its collection of balls, picks up the new piece, and eats it, then retrieves the load and carries it to the next ball I have just thrown out. Once again it repeats the same performance. Finally, having eaten the last ball, the jay gathers up the load for the last time and flies away with it. To test whether or not the behavior is just a haphazard reaction, when it returns I make the bird repeat the same sequence of actions a number of times. But not once, either to eat another morsel thrown at its feet or to start another collection, does the jay leave its original load and forget it.

They place their nest in the very top of the tallest spruce standing by the lakeshore. From this splendid elevation every approach from east and west, from north and south, is wide open. This is the way the kingbirds like it—wide visibility. They accept no environment where enemies can sneak up on them from cover. Out in the open it must be, where they can face the world and all its dangers.

Here between heaven and earth the kingbirds move freely. Here under the splendor of the blue sky they perform their circling, fluttering, and ceremonial flights, be it to demonstrate impressively against the intrusion of whoever dares approach their high domain or to display their emotional reactions to mate, nest, and offspring.

The kingbirds seal the choice of their nest site by crowding together into the small space between the topmost spikes of the spruce and there engage in excited wing-flutterings accompanied by loud crisp *kritch-kritch-kritch* notes repeated in rapid succession.

The nest-building itself is a rite of passion. The female is the chief actor. As if pretending the burden overwhelms her, she carries aloft in an excited fluttering flight a long trailing dead grass. For a moment she hovers above the spruce top, her white breast shining, her tail with its white crossband fanned. She drops the precious stuff into the spruce top. It sticks to the leaves. She descends upon it and with enthusiastic exaggerated movements she scratches the dead straw with her feet and molds it with her breast, balancing herself during this animated activity upon her widespread wings. When she has finished she lifts on mincing wings straight up from the spruce top, sounding her shrill twittering. Then off she flies to fetch another long strand of dead grass and attaches this to the spruce top by the same ritual procedure.

Five days later the result is a messy collection of dead grasses

draped down the sides of the spruce top with spears of unsub-
dued stiff stalks sticking out in all directions. But the depression
in the center appears to be strictly according to specifications.
The kingbird hovers over it, sinks down into it, and sits there
with a proud mien looking out over her wide world. The next
two days she devotes to giving the construction the finishing
touches. She pulls hanging strands over the edge of the nest cup
and tucks them in. From below, the nest now appears to be
solid, roomy, and comparatively tidy.

The male's contributions to the nest-building rites are essentially limited to just being there, to escorting the transporation
of materials, and to his own displays, flights, circling and twit-

terings, emphasizing and amplifying hers. At the first break of dawn he sings a song dedicated to him and to her alone, a brief high-pitched sequence that ends on two *ee-yah* notes, as unexpected and as musically perfect a dawn song as only a flycatcher can deliver.

On a beautiful summer morning, when the dew suspended from the short spruce leaves in glistening drops is struck by the slanted beams of the rising sun, the kingbird drops her first egg into the spruce-top nest. I know the exact moment, for I can see her raising herself slightly, not in order to leave the nest, but to sit down again upon her elevated throne, tranquil and aloof.

Presently she lifts from the nest straight into the air, and the male, leaving his observation post nearby, joins her on vibrating wings. Their twittering in unison sounds like the small crackling noises of a fire . The egg is there, it is exposed. The nest, no longer empty and waiting, is full of life, full of meaning and the future.

With each day that passes, with each egg that appears in the bottom of the nest, the kingbirds become noisier, more excitable and belligerent. The mere sight of a crow or a raven or a jay, their avowed enemies, even from distances of half a mile, brings the kingbirds to the attack. Before the kingbirds' stinging assault the large black raven ponderously rolls over and over in midair, his ragged wings flapping. The flycatcher furies have difficulty to decide which is up and which is down and where to aim their spearing. During this period of high nervous tension nobody is safe from the kingbird's wrath—not even previously tolerated quite harmless neighbors, especially if, like the red-winged blackbird, they show the slightest resemblance to a crow. At the sounding of the alarm both kingbirds go to the attack, the female leaving the nest in a state of high excitement. The deafening screams and the ferocity of their charge as they wheel and dive upon the intruder, often landing on its back, pecking it and chasing it out of the premises, attract the attention of all within sight. For a critical moment the nest and its con-

[169]

tents are at the mercy of the wide open world. But there is protection in the kingbirds' highly specialized and exaggerated aggressiveness, because the ostentation of their hue and cry diverts
attention from the nest and in this way usually preserves it
intact.

During incubation the kingbirds seldom leave the nest unat-
tended. The male is alert to every move the female makes and
rarely misses the moment when she decides to take a recess. He
appears as she leaves and they exchange chirping notes as they
meet. The nest with its contents holds them together, absorbs
most of their reactions. Looking down from his high post, the
male every so often gazes at the eggs, turning upon them first
one eye, then the other. All is well—I see the verdict in his cool
pose. The female returns, and as she turns the eggs over with
her bill she twitters softly.

Across the bay a little over half a mile south of the kingbirds'
nest, a pair of pigeon hawks are occupied with raising a brood
of three on top of a large flat nest in a white pine. They, too,
have a wide view over the land. Like the kingbirds, they are also
a noisy couple who jealously guard their own and screech their
piercing protests against the approach of any creature larger
than themselves, be it bird or man.

It may seem surprising that in the close proximity of so no-
torious a small bird killer as the pigeon hawk the highly exposed kingbirds are still among the living. But there are reasons.
In nature a protective tendency is often opposed against a haz-
ard, a compensatory indemnity against a sacrifice. Too great
pressure is not often maintained in any one direction. The kingbirds' territory is small as compared to the falcons' larger one
that stretches over at least a square mile. Within such an expanse the prey possibilities are manifold. Luck and chance select
for the falcons the easiest victims, the ones taken by surprise,
the injured ones that cannot escape quickly enough, the ones
whose watchfulness is not constantly at peak level, those whose
skill in the art of concealment is not up to par.

Under these circumstances, for all their conspicuousness, the odds against the kingbirds' falling prey to the falcons are rather good. The impetuosity of their defense repudiates their exhibitionism. Ferocity is not always commensurate with size in the interplay of avian hazards and hostilities. The advantages of strong threat and attack on the part of an aggressor often impose retreat as the best way out for the opponent, however superior he may be. Thus, in encounters with the defenders when trespassing upon the kingbirds' premises, the falcons usually choose flight and beat a retreat as inoffensively as do the large black ravens.

The nestlings are two days old and I sit peacefully waiting for the return of the female, due soon from a foraging expedition. She arrives, and like a bolt from the blue sky the female pigeon hawk swoops down upon her. This is not the first time I have seen the hawk make a successful assault on a parent bird near the nest, for when the parent is focusing its attention on the nest and is possessed by the powerful drive to attend its young, it is at a great disadvantage. At that moment all the cards are stacked against the kingbird, for this time the falcon is out in quest of prey not easily denied her. How the kingbird escapes her lightning dash and outstretched talons is a breathless miracle. But the kingbird's sharp watchfulness and her instantaneous dexterity of movement as she drops away like a stone and disappears save her life.

The impetus of the falcon's tremendous élan as she misses the kingbird brings her up short clutching the rim of the nest, her wings spread out over its sides. There she sits with the sun shining upon the beautiful golden-brown shades of her plumage, her big eyes gleaming in the fierce-looking face with its hooked beak, magnificent in her defeat.

Like a fury the male kingbird is at her, screaming in fear and defiance. He dashes at the head of the falcon. She ducks to avoid his violent onslaught. She half sprawls over the nest, the tiny young utterly at her mercy. But at this moment the falcon's hunting role is played out temporarily and the kingbird, strong, fast, ruthless, indefatigable, gives her no quarter. She releases her clutch upon the nest sagging under her weight and torn by her talons. She departs under the wings and the feet and the bill of the kingbird, fiercely pursued, routed out of the neighborhood.

A minute or two later the female kingbird returns. She examines the nest, she stands over it. And as she stands there and utters her soft chirping notes and as she settles to brood, she dispels my fears and relieves my suspense. If I entertained any doubts at that desperate moment of attack about her survival, she now gives me irrefutable proof that she herself is alive and that her young ones are safe.

CHAPTER NINE

The Southeastern Slope

We met after her chicks hatched and I never knew the spot where the ruffed grouse hid her eggs and sat on them. She was a beautiful bird of the red plumage phase, rare in these parts. I have only seen three of them, two with reddish ruffs and this one. Her small black ruff and the tail's broken black crossband contrasted nicely with the rusty-red ground color of the rest of her plumage.

In the early spring the cock that belongs to this family was on his drumming log slightly off the crest of the hill that forms the backbone of the southeastern slope. The setting was perfect. The log was rotted red and partly covered with a soft mat of emerald-green moss. The drooping branches of a half-grown spruce supplied a suitable backdrop. A row of light brown droppings marked the path of the cock's strutting to and fro and a ray of sunlight filtered through the foliage upon the finely drawn pencil lines and shadings of the bird's gray-phase plumage.

Slowly, with an elaborate, proudly revealing gesture that seemed to say, "Look what I've got here," the cock opened his white-tipped gray tail with the black unbroken band across it. As a prelude to a few strutting steps he made forward nodding movements with his head and shook his voluminous black ruff so that it stood like a large collar around his head and neck. His crest was on end and his body feathers fluffed, and he looked much larger than he actually was. He opened his wings partly and their tips trailed on the log. He twisted the stiff primaries so that their ends turned inward and slightly forward to form a hollow like a scoop. With spasmodic movements the cock began to beat his wings in the air, but the movements were too slow to produce any sound. Quickly their speed increases and sound comes, *thump—thump*, faster, louder, *thurrrump*, and the drumming rolls on in a fantastic pauseless rhythm ending abruptly with a gloriously triumphant *whirrrrrr*.

The stillness afterward was anticlimactic. The cock's feathers fell back into place, the fan of the tail closed. He relaxed and stood motionless on the red log. Then once again he slowly unfolded the beautiful arch of his banded tail and with utter deliberation and slow measured movements he went through the preliminaries in exactly the prescribed order. Again his wings began their thumping ordinance, soundlessly at first, then increasing in velocity and resonance to its final climax.

But now the courtship of the ruffed grouse is long since over. The sun comes through the foliage from a different angle and the cock is no longer on the red log. The female, who at that time heard him and came forward to him, is in front of me lying on her side in a heap of fine sand that the rains washed down the slope, dusting it through her relaxed plumage. Grouped around her are six of the cock's progeny, small downy chicks hardly more than a week old, kicking up the dust with their tiny scratching feet.

I arrive upon this lovely scene a little too suddenly and it dissolves in a flash. With crest on end and ruff flared the female

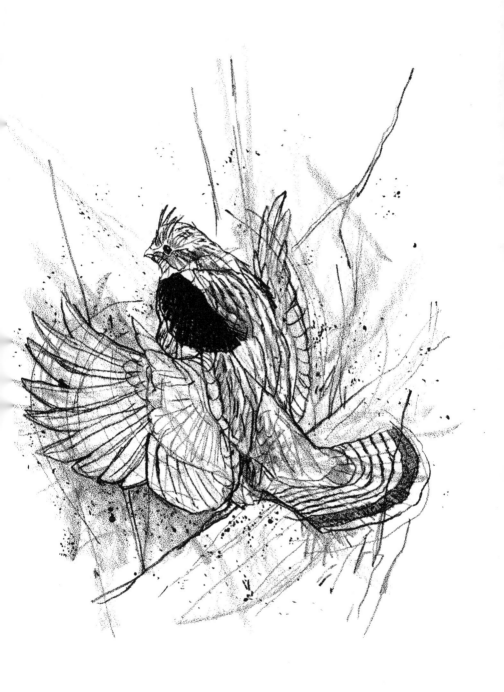

flies at me in an onrush so violent it makes me reel. Less than two feet from me she flops to the ground, whining like a small hurt dog. All the chicks scatter and press their tiny speckled bodies tight to the safe earth, seeking its protection. The mother about faces and with wings and tail spread wide runs crouching over the dead leaves, awkwardly trailing the tip of her left wing asymmetrically.

A small movement not far away, seen out of the corner of my eye, fixes my attention on a spot where I presently discern the shape of a chick half hidden under a green leaf. I am curious to see what is going to happen next, so I remain "frozen" beside the chick at a little distance from the female, who stopped when she found no one following her. Gradually the distance and my stillness combine to wipe my image from the slate of her awareness and she stretches her neck, casting a questioning, distrustful look about her. It takes a long time for her to become reassured—five and a half minutes pass (the watch is in my hand) before the all-clear message penetrates her senses. Then, very gingerly, she begins to move one step at a time, her foot lifted high and hesitatingly lest the earth upon which she walks cannot be trusted, until she finally regains her normal gait. At this point her ruffed feathers fall flat against her body. Popping her head forward with each measured step, she looks and clucks. Soft cheeping noises, the gentle rustle of small feet running over the debris of the forest floor give her immediate answer, and I see six rows of rippled movement worming through the undercover, all converging upon the clucking hen.

All I heard in the spring was the quaint nasal note, *pëent-pëent;* to my great disappointment, though watching and waiting at dusk and at dawn, I neither saw nor heard the famous courtship flight of the woodcock.

The hen is as secretive about her nest as the ruffed grouse. I crisscross nearly every foot of the slope with its thousand and one hiding places in an effort to find it. A movement would reveal her, but she never moves. I imagine how she sits motionless relying upon her protective coloring to make her almost invisible among the brownish shades of her surroundings, watching, awaiting the noisy approach of the monster closing in upon her privacy. But my steps apparently do not take me close enough to the tight little area around her, designated as the limits within which she cannot allow anyone, to shake her confidence in her own safety.

After the chicks hatch she is a changed creature. The train of precocious downy youngsters at her heels requires quite a different kind of behavior. Time and again when least expected she explodes under my feet. Although after the first warning I keep constantly on the alert for her, I never manage to avoid being taken by surprise. She has two different kinds of display

with which she meets me. One features the onrush, the flop down, and the running away with one wing trailing, very similar to the show the grouse puts on, and a degree less highly motivated than the second display. This is a fantastic exhibition of exaggerated movements performed in midair in full view of the "enemy." Suddenly the woodcock rises to a height of about six feet, her wings flapping wildly and producing a penetrating whistling noise, her landing gear down and rocking. She remains thus suspended in midair, flapping, rocking, whistling for about half a minute, then drops like a stone obliquely back into the undergrowth.

The behavior of the chicks is no less remarkable. As most precocious birdlings are apt to do in moments of danger, they scatter, but with one additional movement of note. Scampering away, they invariably lift their baby wings high above their backs as if preparing for an immediate takeoff without the vestige of a stiff pinion feather to support such a rash intention. But the lifted wing is always full of meaning. The movements of birds as well as their songs and calls convey direct communications that are sometimes symbolic, at other times ritualized. The lifted wing, while it sometimes shows an intention to take flight, in certain situations, also expresses hostility and aggression, and in defense it suggests appeasement. The tiny woodcocks' display of the lifted wings fits into the last situation; it is a gesture of utter abandon, an eloquent plea for the one chance of escape.

At the foot of the southeastern slope overlooking the lake there is a rock whose surface is faulted. This creates flat places between the ridges. Nothing grows on the rock except grasses that like a dry environment and a few straggly stalks of bush honey-suckle that find a foothold in the meager soil deposited between the wrinkles of the rock. This is the place dedicated to the whippoorwills' courtship.

As dusk gathers and deepens one of the birds arrives in a wheeling flight, looking like a giant shadowy moth. The flash of white tail feathers tells me it is the male. He alights and crouches beside one of the ridges. With a clucking note, *chuck*, similar to the clicking on of the power before the start of a resonant radio transmission, the bird turns on his loud-speaker.

The hour of the whippoorwills' evening concert is at hand. Two of them begin calling in the distance, one far away across the lake, the other one closer, from across Little Bay. Their songs float from echo to echo in the transparent night and mingle with the almost deafening rhythmic harangues of the bird there in front of me on the rock. And their singing fills nature's hall of splendid acoustics: *chuck*—whipp*poor*will, *chuck* —WHIPP*poor*WILL!

Suddenly the bird on the rock greatly accelerates the rhythm of its calling. The cause is the arrival of the female; the male must have heard her, sensed her approach, long before I did. Out of the night she wheels overhead, all shadowy, without a spot of white on her tail, and the sight of her sharply cuts off the male's breathless singing. She wobbles in the air, flops down beside him, and the sudden silence stands around them as a protecting wall guarding their privacy. Gently the birds nudge each other. One of them springs into the air and comes down on the other side of the mate. The partner repeats the performance, a flirtatious nightly game of whippoorwill musical chairs. Sitting close together, the two birds carry on a soft cooing conversation.

Out of the dusk a third whippoorwill appears and disrupts the cosy tête-à-tête. With one accord the pair take to the air and a wheeling pursuit develops. No passion, no swift movements are involved in these activities. All of them are soft and airy, measured in rhythm, wheeling and flapping with shadowy wings, owl-like, among the trees, accompanied by short notes and cooing sounds, *cooorah—cooorah*. Then two of the wheeling shadows vanish from the scene and the cock, left alone, flops down upon the rock and feels moved to deliver fifty-two *chuck*—whipp*poor*wills without a stop.

At that count the remarkable change in tempo of the cock's

recital occurs again. The female's approach, her presence, her nearness send the male into a frenzy of agitation that lasts until she alights beside him. He interrupts his loud fast calls and I hear soft, soft, cooing notes. The altered mood expressed in their muted calling belongs to the summer's night and to their proximity. And all this, their graceful ceremonies and their varied utterances, engenders the growing intimacy and dependency between them that are to guarantee the survival of the species and their own replacement when eventually their day, their night, is done.

But the place the whippoorwill female chooses to deposit her eggs is on a northern slope. There in a dark secluded spot under the towering evergreens, sparsely canopied by the dry twigs of a fallen spruce, the two eggs, blotched with light brown, lie on a thin bed of pine leaves surrounded by a mass of white open-faced bunchberry blossoms. All day she sits on the eggs, continuously if left undisturbed, her eyes half closed, asleep. At dusk the male's first call signaling his emergence from the day roost awakens her. After that, in the darkness, the two shining eggs become the rallying point around which two pairs of luminous red lanterns attached to nearly indistinguishable forms move, vanish, and return again.

As the light strikes it from different angles when he turns, hovers, or retreats in flight, the color of the male's throat patch shifts from night-black to ruby-red. Like a jeweled pendulum in rapid propulsion from one apex through a dip almost sweeping the ground to the other, the ruby-throated hummingbird performs his spectacular courtship flight before his partner in a little dale on the east side of the southeastern slope. Anon his pace reaches such a velocity that the fine whine of a high-pitched speed-note mingles with his continuous *chitter*ing vocalizations.

The female in her demure olive-green dress delicately fans her tail adorned with a row of white pearly dots at the end. She is concerned with nothing but probing with her fine curved bill and darting tongue for the nectar contained in the modest chalices of the early blooming buffalo-berry bush. After accomplished probing she sits lightly on a little twig just above the roof of the just-unfolded sarsaparilla. She looks this way and that, sees nothing that excites her, gives herself a little shake, and preens the feathers under her left wing. The male dips before her closer and closer and closer.

Suddenly her mood changes. She sees the male and reacts with elfin fervor to his oscillating dance of adulation, her whole being responding to the implied proposal. She dashes into his flight pattern. And he, as if released from a form of ritual movement, however splendidly designed, dashes after her. Like two darts the pair vanish into the green foliage.

I find her again a few days later. Now it is she who is performing the pendulum act, not up and down and up again but sideways strictly in the horizontal plane. The hapless butt of her obvious displeasure is the purple finch that also lives on the slope. The midget fury buzzes about the ears of the bewildered trespasser, and it is easy to guess the reason why. Hunching its shoulders, the finch tries in vain to follow the movements of its wee buzzing adversary, then finally gives up and quickly withdraws out of reach. The hummingbird looks about, hovers, *chitters*, a note of released tension, then darts away, mission accomplished.

The knoblike beautifully camouflaged nest is placed like a saddle across the horizontal branch of a young white birch standing halfway up the slope near the edge of a group of evergreens. What would some birds do, I wonder, without the spiders and their glistening gossamer threads that visibly or invisibly in such profusion drape every nook and corner of the forest? The hummingbird's thimbleful of fluffy plant down and fine lichens is plastered and molded and anchored to the branch with this incredibly tough and clean adhesive to make of it a masterpiece of solid lightness. The female hovers high above the nest, cautiously looking right and left. She flips her tail, flashing its row of "pearls," and then lets herself airily down by stages into the dainty nest cup. With small movements of adjustment she feels for the two pea-sized eggs. And as she cuddles them warmly against her bare brood patch she abandons herself to a session of peace and repose, her tail and head at jaunty angles above the rim of the nest.

Many other birds also live on the hospitable southeastern slope. Yellow-shafted flickers, downy woodpeckers, yellow-bellied sapsuckers, and hairy woodpeckers, one pair of each species, find ample room there to conduct their slightly diverging activities without getting into one another's feathers.

About thirty years ago the large poplar stub in the south

corner of the slope harbored the nest of a pair of flickers for the first time. From then on it became a tower of refuge, a stub of extended flicker tradition, as is so often the case with these inviting old broken-off dead poplar trunks in the untouched forest. To this stub the same pair of flickers returned every year until the demise of one or both of them. After that the survivor with a new mate, or a new pair, inherited the stub. One year a pair of pileated woodpeckers succumbed to the attraction of the flicker stub and imposed themselves upon the premises before the flickers' return. Finding themselves homeless upon arrival, the flickers wandered about for several days in a state of intense frustration. However, when for some reason the large unwanted squatter abandoned the started hole and went elsewhere to nest, the flickers, no longer homeless, quickly regained their composure, took over the hole with the oval doorway, finished it, and raised therein their own family.

In the course of time doorways leading to a zigzagging complex of cavities pockmarked the stub. Eventually dry rot broke down the walls between two of these nest holes, providing the current tenants with a double-entrance apartment. But this arrangement turned out to have fatal consequences when a red squirrel took the occupant by surprise through the undefended opening at the rear and in due time emptied the nest of its contents.

When the girth of a stub is geared to the size of smaller birds the downy woodpeckers follow closely the flickers' taste in nest-tree selection. With them also stub tradition plays an important role, and it is interesting to see how the addition of holes year after year increases the attraction of the slowly rotting stub until its final collapse. Sometimes this happens so suddenly that the bird inside is trapped and killed.

The other two woodpeckers—the hairy woodpecker and the yellow-bellied sapsucker—make their choices along slightly different lines. With them the quality of their hole-boring equipment exercises a deciding influence. The hairy woodpecker, therefore, in possession of a massive bill and a strongly constructed neck, to a marked extent chooses live trees in preference to dead stubs, while the sapsucker with its less formidable excavation tool is more likely to choose live trees well past their prime, or dead stubs. The quality of the wood and the condition of the core are also important. The poplar with its soft wood is the nest tree best liked by both species. And the fact that both woodpeckers are given to excavating a number of trial holes that are never used suggests that a certain amount of searching goes on before the birds can settle upon a tree with, presumably, the best kind of inner core wood in which a cavity can be most successfully excavated.

The four species of woodpeckers also show similarly slight differences in their food tastes and food-gathering methods. The flickers prefer ants over and above all other foods and their curved bills and long darting tongues are well adapted for pulling these insects out of their galleries and burrows. The downy woodpeckers take small stuff, spiders and flying insects and other minor things that hide and hibernate in the nooks and corners under the bark of the twigs and branches of the trees. Grubs and caterpillars of larger size and succulent fatness, found deep in tree trunks and rotting stubs, appeal to the hairy woodpeckers, while the sapsuckers, particularly when flying insects, such as moths and mayflies or the large shiny carpenter ants, are scarce or nonexistent, suck the sap of the trees from rows of bored sap wells.

Under these circumstances the adjustment of the four closely related woodpeckers to one another's presence is exemplary. No need for pugnacity among next-door neighbors who do not compete with one another for food and nest sites. On occasion two or three of these woodpeckers may even set up house at no greater distance from each other than fifteen to twenty-five feet. The limits for their mutual tolerance are usually marked at the edge of a circle with a radius of some fifteen to thirty feet around respective nest trees, with individual concessions arranged between pairs nesting very close together. Their ranges, the space each pair uses mainly for foraging and resting, are superimposed upon one another and can be traversed at will without protest or interference. Only the intrusion of an outsider belonging to any of the four species upsets the harmony of the woodpecker group. With the males opposing the trespassing males and the females pitted against females, such an intruder invariably meets with swift and uncompromising response from its counterparts in residence.

To distinguish the least flycatcher from its close relative, the alder flycatcher, merely by color and field marks is difficult, sometimes impossible. The two are best separated by their voices and by the type of environment in which they are found, although the latter is not always entirely reliable as on occasion both have taken up residence on the southeastern slope. But their songs—the least flycatcher's *chebec* and the alder flycatcher's *fitzbee* (as it is pronounced in these parts)—if such these unmusical raspy utterances can be called, are so typical that once heard they cannot be forgotten or confused.

Other things also distinguish the least flycatcher and set it apart: the way it sits on the twig upright, its twinkling eye that because of the light-colored eye-ring appears more prominent than it is, the characteristic tremulous movements of wings and tail as the bird alights on its perch or on the rim of the nest or as the male jerks his head to add emphasis to each of his clipped *chebecs*. The least flycatcher seems unable to do anything without the accompaniment of vocal expression. The male likes to interpolate his pursuit activities with wheezy exclamations of *gee-whizz-whizz* and he never approaches his mate or comes to feed her on the nest without whispering a breathy *thrrr-thrr-thrrr*. The female continuously conducts with herself a private conversation, muttering softly *pit-pit* every time she hops or feeds or gets off or on the nest, or for that matter does anything that she feels requires vocal adjections.

The environment that satisfies the taste of the least flycatcher has a green room between the roof of the undergrowth and the canopy of a younger generation of leafy trees that is warm, light, and airy, the same kind of surroundings that flying insects like. This room also has conveniently exposed perches not too high and not too low, from which the bird can make its fly-catching sorties. Many-pronged crotches and other suitable nest sites must be available at middling heights to which the least flycatcher's neatly fashioned nest can be securely lashed with cobweb and other sticky stuff.

The slope's southernmost corner, a triangular piece of land bounded by the road on one side and by the lakeshore on the other, adequately provides all this, and in the rather constricted area seven pairs of least flycatchers carve out among themselves a mosaic of territories. The smallest and most favored lots are tightly circumscribed, allowing each pair not more than enough space in which to find a supply of food and suitable nest sites.

Those on the periphery are larger and their borders are less sharply delineated, at least on the one or two sides where no pressure from a neighboring least flycatcher exists and the owner is allowed some expansion, usually into less favored surroundings.

Being a small bird with specialized habits and needs, the least flycatcher is best served with the compact allotment of land. He is not given to large movements except in migration. In his small territory he effectively isolates himself and his mate from his own species. Privacy is to him a condition for the successful raising of a family. With his harsh little cough of a song he proclaims his presence to the neighbors and holds them at bay. Belligerency is his best form of attack, vigilance his best defense, and with these two qualities prominently represented in his character he keeps the borders of his domain rigidly outlined and intact. He cannot afford to be meek. His mode of life and the niche nature assigned to him render harmonious coexistence with his own kind impossible.

Along the lakeshore an abandoned sapsucker cavity high up in a now-dead poplar with free and easy access direct from the open lake appeals to a pair of metal-blue tree swallows. From their swift foraging flights high and low over the lake, with occasional dips marked by widening rings in the water, the pair sweep in to the hole together. They examine it, they cling to its doorway side by side, and their soft-toned exchange of notes, *pritt-tritt-pritt-tritt*, involves no one but themselves. Significant secret intentions are here being formulated and developed that in due time will end in nest-building, egg laying, and a nestful of young swallows with enormous mouths that will readily receive everything the parents are able to catch and pop into them.

In the midst of the least-flycatcher territories, two black-capped chickadees, he and she, some time ago converted a five-foot birch stub into a softly lined nursery excavated deeply into the rotting wood. Here, with special attention paid to movements and behavior in order to preserve the utmost measure of secrecy, the pair are now zealously attending to the welfare and safety of their brood of five.

At various heights, and spread out over the slope, mud nests serve three pairs of robins in adjoining territories. With them, through the vagaries of open-nest fortunes and misfortunes, the nesting season is a succession of nest-building ever and anon to replace used nests or plundered nests or deserted nests. To make four or five unsuccessful nesting attempts is for them common practice. The choice of nest site, the opportunity of the predator are based largely on chance and no amount of solicitude and watchfulness can ever entirely circumvent all the risks connected with the robins' nesting. But neither failure nor success greatly disrupts the equilibrium or the protracted flow of the nesting cycles of these handsome red-breasted thrushes. With blissful proclivity for living in and for the moment, they follow easily the rhythmical sequences of events and with inimitable detachment perform whatever is set out for them to do; and their capacity for producing many broods in a season takes care of their linear succession.

The brilliant flash of the scarlet tanager—how many times have I witnessed his specialized defense strategy around the nest openly saddling the longest branch of the balsam fir just above the marigold ponds! Could anything more vividly symbolize his aggressive intent than the color of this bird as he dramatically projects himself like a bolt of fire upon the unwary trespasser! No need here for spectacular attitudes and ostentatious displays. The sudden flash of red is a deterrent strong enough to force the immediate retreat of any surprised intruder whatever the reason for its unwarranted presence.

The scarlet tanager's artful aggressive dodge is not unequivocally aimed at the protection of the nest. The red male is an asset and for his own safety he enjoys a phenomenal ability to keep himself invisible among the foliage of the treetops. But his conspicuousness also makes him a liability and his exposure in the vicinity of the nest adds in some measure to its risks.

Nest-building and incubation belong to the female tanager and in relation to nest security her subdued greenish coloring compensates nicely for the hazards that the male's vividness creates. The tanagers' problem of nest protection has also another aspect. The male's tendency to escort the female on her excursions in search of nesting materials and food, a habit he shares with some of the finches among other birds, leaves the nest without surveillance for more or less prolonged periods during which anything can happen. The condition that could offset this situation, the well-concealed nest, is, as in this case, not always fulfilled. The good and the bad, the advantageous and the unprofitable, are well intermixed in the workings of nature and chance is a mighty element. The main principle of all nature's operation is the poised balance.

I have here passed in review some of the most common and most interesting birds that many years ago lived and nested on the southeastern slope in one single season. But they are only a small part of the recorded hundred-odd birds of thirty-four species whose no less than fifty nests, found or presumed to be there, were crowded into the densely populated south corner of these benign two or three acres of land in that memorable year.

The southeastern slope is the most remarkable place in our forest. We happened to build our house there without any deep understanding of its meaning and potentialities. I simply wanted to realize an ardent wish to awaken in the morning for the rest of my life with the sunrise in my face. Moreover, exposure to the east and the south would make the house lighter and warmer, especially in winter, in this northern land. Only gradually in the course of the years I have come to realize how truly in accordance with the tendencies of all the life around us this impulse was.

The combination of the lake and the rise of the land which gives shelter from the north winds and the prevailing westerlies creates the unsurpassed attraction of the slope for the birds. Here is the sunrise with its gift of early light and warmth, and the water with its reflections and its humidity, the prime promoters of growth and wild life. Here, in the spring, the migrants from the south are tempted to end their long flight in the hospitable embrace of this sheltering land. Here the birds going south again in the fall follow closely along the shore and the sloping contour. The southeastern slope is to the naturalist the privileged piece of land above all others, full of promise of sustained interest where amazing things happen and no situation is implausible.

Dawn is the hour when each bird on this slope stands to be counted by voice in a roll call unequaled in symphonic composition. This is the awakening when the first bird notes fall upon the air, separate and distinct. The author of the opening bars varies. Sometimes the forest's most inveterate night singer, the olive-backed thrush, makes night into day at the break of dawn with its deep-toned rolling mounting theme; or the whippoorwill sounds its last ringing call, ready to give up its nocturnal reign; or the nighthawk makes its last booming dive over the lake before going to roost on the flat branch in the tall poplar.

But listen, suddenly the first songs of the robin float down from the top of the spruce with gentle ease, liquid and full-throated. A song sparrow answers from below with three staccato notes followed by an elaborate warble, a splendid loud rendition from a minikin source. A little farther away the fluted strophes of the wood thrush come, with strangely ventriloquial effect as if two birds were engaged in a duet—but there is only one.

Weird explosive noises emanate from the forest floor. Absorbed in a series of lively and mysterious rites three pairs of veeries create wild ripples through the low growth. Swift shadows pass to and fro across the path in the dim light, and their movements are punctuated by harsh discordant notes tossed from bird to bird. For a moment the slightly melancholy recitation of a white-throated sparrow with rhetorical emphasis interrupts the thrushes' conversation. One of the veeries comes into view, mounts a low twig, and with its bill wide open ejaculates a short strident note. And then at last, having thus prepared the world for what is to follow, the thrush begins to sing, softly at first, softly as in a whisper, the descending cadences infinitely clear and distinct, tinkling in quality, then louder but never departing from the temperance of delivery that is the vocal trademark of the thrush. Anon, without cause or reference, a short harsh note breaks into the harmonies, an experiment in contrast that does nothing but enhance the veery's main motif.

The dawn chorus swells in volume. The five red-eyed vireos, scattered across the slope, with their fifty to sixty songs a minute beautifully mellowed by the different distances from which they are delivered, provide a continuous accompaniment as these birds meander through the crowns of the trees. A ruby-crowned kinglet emerges from a group of conifers where his nest is going to be and in easy stages flies down to the spruce by the lakeshore and back up again, stopping to deliver his prolonged full-toned songs at regular intervals. An ovenbird, having pronounced three loud versions of his territorial theme, suddenly goes aloft in a flight-song of such ecstatic quality that his voice is momentarily lost from pure fervor. The songs of ten warblers delivering their contributions from favorite song perches, some sibilant like the black-throated green's, others warbling like the magnolia's, and still others rhythmic, rippling, like the Canada warbler's, are repeated over and over again. In a valiant attempt to assert his own importance in the face of such a welter of contestants, the chipping sparrow adds his trilled phrase to the warblers' songs with protracted insistence. Two purple finches in full magenta attire hold forth from the tops of two balsam firs in a coloratura recital of rare virtuosity and length, inspired by mutual competition. And now, with all this splendid diversity of songs and pronouncements receding to mere background music, the rose-breasted grosbeak lets his own notes drop into the dawn chorus, full and honey-sweet, with the perfect detachment of the acknowledged soloist.

The singing mounts, swells, maintains itself triumphantly for fifteen or twenty minutes at a volume it will not reach again until another dawn. Then the birds fall to feeding; the breaking of the fast can be put off no longer. The singing dies down, but there is no total silence. Songs and call notes from this multitude of birds constantly interrupt their feeding, the period of their matutinal activities is at its height. Then once again the singing intensifies, magnifies. But the business of the full day impinges upon the songsters and provides too much distraction. The vocal self-expressions of the birds fluctuate irregularly until a midafternoon low spreads virtual silence throughout the forest. But then again, just before roosting time, and for some —the thrushes, the ovenbirds, the winter wrens—continuing far into the night as a last echo of the dawn chorus, a resurgence of song plays heavenly though disjointed music to the sunset and to the rising moon and the stars.

All this was long ago. It is no longer the same. The southeastern slope is still where it was, a sunlit and warm place even in winter when a paler sun reflects its lesser radiance upon the snow and the rocks, where the forest growth is still luscious and where in summer insect life abounds. But there have been great changes. And man and his impact upon the earthly environment must bear no small part of the responsibility for the significant alterations that are gradually coming to light in the character of the birdlife of today.

CHAPTER TEN

The Great Disaster

It is springtime and a day in the second week of May. The trembling aspen, always the earliest of all the trees, is coming into leaf. The violet-tinted birches stand prettily decorated with pendulous ripe staminate catkins and their tightly folded new leaves look like green dots peeping from the shiny brown bracts. The juneberry is enveloped in a cloud of bloom sending its delicate fragrance out over the neighborhood. But the red cherry with its buds looking like miniature pingpong balls stuck to needle-thin stems is not yet in any hurry to start the opening ceremonies. Along the overflow of the spring and around the ponds, the marsh marigolds have already burst into opulent flowering, two or three wake-robins nod their red heads beside the path, and a spread of goldthreads lift starlike ingenue faces on stems sprung from their golden rootlets embedded in the moist green moss.

Into this hopeful environment the first two least flycatchers arrive and I am sure neither is a stranger. The way they act, the

song perches they select, the localities they assign for their respective centers of activity tell me that they nested here last year and perhaps even a year or two before that. Apart from this, first come, first served, and without further ado they indicate their intention to establish themselves on two lots right in the middle of the southeastern triangle. Without marked emphasis or enthusiasm they pronounce their short-cut songs; there is nothing yet to be particularly emphatic about. For the most part they catch flies, flying out into the air and back to the perch, and the snapping sound produced by their bills is quite audible. They are hungry and a little weary from the last lap of the journey from the south, and the sun shining through the trees brings out numbers of edible mites.

During the next few days more least flycatchers arrive, all males. They see the others there; they recognize the light places, the green room, find the convenient flycatching perches and other things to their liking. They may be young birds without any special goal, so why not stay! The two birds that arrived first are not altogether agreeable to this turn of events and they begin to resist unauthorized movements across the land on which they settled first. At this stage their arguments are conducted mainly by songs given from strategic points with a greater emphasis, a jerk of the head and trembling of the tail, telling the newcomers with so many curt notes to keep off the green grass. Still more least flycatchers arrive until there are seven of them. Apparently this is a case of the compelling attraction of the crowd to which not only birds are apt to succumb. And so each of them carves out for himself a piece of territory that holds what he needs for living and nesting.

This puts much more zest and excitement into the flycatcher situation. Competition between the seven males becomes very sharp because not quite enough space is available to accommodate so many flycatchers so close together on choice lots. The result is highly intensified aggressive behavior. Bulletlike pursuits reinforce the birds' vocal challenges and easily develop into breast-to-breast battles with the two combatants falling to the ground, separating, and whizzing off each to his own premises. This in turn results in sharper delineation of the properties, so that even I can tell rather precisely through which shrub, at which rock, A's territory touches upon B's and where B's land ends and C's begins.

Competition is fine in many ways, but too much creates tension. And when the nervous tension fundamental to any kind of living increases beyond a certain measure, it produces stress. Now stress within limits is also in the nature of things and gives an edge to living as nothing else can, always provided it is kept within bounds. But as the flycatcher situation develops, it is soon clear that the problem of too many birds in one place is going to arise. I detect the mounting tension in the birds' lightning movements, in the shaking of their tails as they voice their challenging songs. I hear it in their breathy *thrrr* notes and observe it in their growing intolerance toward birds of other species, behavior often associated with stress among birds and other creatures. The proper balance between the environment and the number of living things that exist therein is remarkably delicate and even a slight imbalance in this relationship seems to have strange effects upon the nervous systems of the inhabitants.

And then the flycatcher female arrives. The encounter with the stranger of his own kind catches the male off balance. He dashes at every bird he sees, crossing territory lines and being chased off; he sings and attacks again. The female's innocent appearance creates a confounded melée, until her soft notes, *pit-pit,* or the way she flits hither and yon, concerned with nothing but herself and the place and perhaps also the song she just heard, suddenly penetrates the male's ken. The next instant he seems stricken by the sight of her; his frenzy drains away; he pounces lightly upon her and bears her to the ground, thus impressing upon her the reality of his presence. She escapes from under him as if nothing had happened, shakes herself, and continues to flit about entirely unperturbed. This act settles the future relationship of the pair, though their full connubial partnership is a gradual affair that develops step by step through their increasing attachment to the premises, the site and the nest, culminating eventually in their recognition of each other as mates.

During this period the excitement on the southeastern slope reaches a peak. It spreads from bird to bird in this densely populated area, from the male flycatchers to the females, from the flycatchers to the tree swallows, the robins, the veeries, the red-eyed vireos, the warblers, involving all those that nest on the slope. The air fills with birdsong, ravishingly beautiful music to the human ear, but in fact replete with egocentric reference originally devised to safeguard the living, the reproducing, the survival of each bird among the many. Excitement is catching. Too much of it plays havoc with secretiveness, with prudence

and wariness. Disturbed by all the exaggerated noises and movements, the pursuits and the fighting, mobs of birds gather
wherever the noise is loudest and the turmoil greatest—as people gather around a sensational accident—to sing, to scold, to
chase each other and to fight among themselves, heedless of the
traditional watchfulness and reserve upon which hinges the
preservation of every single bird's life. And the predators gain a
great deal of gratuitous information.

But this is only part of the story. The tension and the stress
have curious effects upon the reactions and the behavior of
nearly all the female flycatchers, with dire consequences to the
success of their nestings.

The noise and excitement created by her mate's frequent engagements with the neighbors greatly disturbs Female C. After
the eggs are in the nest tucked between a low branch and the
trunk of a slender birch she cannot bring herself to sit on them
more than five or ten minutes at a time. She flutters off and on,
repeating *pit-wit, pit-wit,* under her breath. When at last she
sits quietly, the male sings and off she flutters, he approaches
with food in the bill and off she flies before he is able to tender
her his offering, and never once does he succeed in feeding her
as the rule of law bids him. She hears him, sees him fighting,
and she dashes off—not to join in the fray, oh, no—but to return immediately and hover above the nest as if to protect it
from whatever dangers might threaten it, alternatively descending upon it, turning around, adjusting the eggs, off again, on
again interminably. Naturally, the victim of such giddy impulses is not destined ever to hatch an egg.

The situation struck Female B in quite a different manner.
Hers is a peripheral territory and she selects for her nest-building the part of it that lies opposite and a little distance away
from the area where her mate is predominantly occupied with
efforts to maintain the integrity of his southwest border. She
gets nowhere with the building of her first nest, because a pair
of robins certainly not immune to the general state of excitement

on the slope raise strong objections to her presence so near their own nest. Their constant interference discourages the flycatcher and finally she gives up the attempt and moves to another place not far away.

The materials of the unfinished nest are conveniently in evidence and she picks it apart and carries the stuff to the new site. She accomplishes this maneuver by making a series of detours that allow her to slip quickly through the back door of the robins' defenses, so to speak. The robins cannot tell, of course, whether the flycatcher is carrying the stuff to or from the vexatious site, and it does not matter anyway because they are getting used to her diffident flutterings to and fro at the same time that they are becoming more deeply involved in their own affairs with a nestful of newly hatched young. What an ameliorating invention habit is!

Repeated maneuvers of arranging and molding and just sitting in the half-finished nest occupy the flycatcher for two days. Then for no apparent reason she abandons the whole thing and devotes a few days entirely to fly-catching. After that she starts her third nest in what seems to be a fine secure berth formed by two branchlets. A piece of loose white birch bark suspended above twirls protectingly over it in the light breeze. In this enterprise she uses all new materials although the second nest is not far away and still intact. But after a period of heavy rains this third nest dissolves and falls to the ground with all the eggs in it.

By this time the season is well advanced; but nothing daunted, the flycatcher forthwith starts to build her fourth nest and completes it in the record short time of four days. After fourteen days of incubation her eggs hatch. Success at last . . . ? But, alas, when the young are four days old all activity around the nest ceases. The intrepid nest-builder has disappeared.

Territory A is a small area placed in the crowded midst of the flycatcher cluster of territories, just large enough to serve the minimum demands of food and shelter of a pair of least fly-catchers during the nesting season. It belongs to the male who arrived first in the spring and it has therefore been fought over and maintained with no small amount of valor and persistence. The female is a bird of placid temperament. Without ado she places her first nest quite openly in the upright top crotch of a young aspen, without any leafy screening except from above. During incubation she spends most of her time on the nest, adopting from the start a schedule of long sessions and very short recesses. The color of her plumage matches almost exactly that of the smooth olive-green stems of the young poplar and as she sits motionless on the nest with her head and tail protruding slightly above the rim, she resembles the sculptured knob of a healed-over wound. Between his territorial engagements her mate never fails to take time out regularly to bring her food, which she accepts sitting deep down in the nest, her head thrown back and wings shivering. Of all the male least-flycatchers I have known, only one other equaled him in atten-tiveness. And all this unobtrusive heed carries the nest success-fully through the fourteenth day of incubation.

At the rate failures are occurring among the flycatchers I have lost faith in their luck and I am delighted and surprised when I see the subdued little female bringing the first diminu-tive meal and daintily transmitting it to the open mouth of her newly hatched chick. How did it ever come to pass!

With this event I enter upon a period of constant worry about the welfare of the nest and these two parent birds, who continue to go about their business of feeding the nestlings and brooding them as if not a danger in the world could touch them. The blessings of innocence! With the hatching of the young the risks of disaster increase threefold because the par-ents' movements around the nest makes it more conspicuous in spite of all secretiveness, and the longer the nestlings survive the more food they demand; to provide it, the parents more fre-quently leave the nest unguarded and open to attack. And even if the parent birds were capable of guarding and defending it effectively, this is not normally written into the behavior codes of small birds like the flycatchers. They can sound the alarm and fuss and flutter, but in accordance with their usefulness and their relative chances of survival the logic of nature rates the life of the adult bird higher than that of the chick, and consequently the latter must not be rashly exposed to danger without certain safeguards.

Every day the probabilities of disaster increase and surely it cannot be avoided. Early in the morning I run out to see what happened during the night, and I am inordinately relieved every time I find the bird sitting high upon her throne looking down at me. By now she is used to me and she was never much worried about me; she does not know what I know and this is perhaps her salvation. Looking back at the day just ended, I marvel that the nest is still intact and consider it a triumph of well-balanced parental care and solicitude amid great odds. The fourteenth day of life for the nestlings dawns, and incredibly the tiny birds are still alive though threatened by so many perils, marauding blue jays, grackles, and crows; tree-climbing squirrels and chipmunks; the sharp-shinned hawk that nests only a quarter of a mile away; and, last but not least, the loss of temperamental balance that leaves every inhabitant of the crowded slope open to abnormal risks. They are climbing up on the rim of their tiny nest cup, now a bit out of shape from accommodating its increasingly vigorous burden for so long. They flap their wings with complete abandon, hop daringly out of the nest and back in again without notion of danger, evil, or death, only of well-being and adventure and exuberance. And then, finally, with the instinctive boldness derived from the purest form of innocence they leave their haven and emerge into the wide open world.

This was the only one of the ten least flycatcher nests I found in the notable year of 1949 that was marked with success. Apart from what happened to the nests of Females C and

B, eggs and young of four nests fell prey to nest robbers. Two females, D and E, fell victim to the hawk. When an eligible and fancy-free companion soon after joined the second widower they flew together to the nest site selected but never used by his first partner. But even this lucky replacement added nothing to the overall nesting success of the flycatchers, for the female kicked out one of the eggs at a moment of intense disturbance, three mysteriously disappeared, and the fifth was infertile.

Pure coincidence may have had something to do, at least in part, with the remarkable decline of the least flycatcher population to one-fourth of its former density that took place after the events I have just related, not only on the slope but in the whole of the Pimisi Bay region. And although theirs was the most spectacular, declines in the populations of other birds also began to be noted. A study of my daily counts and breeding censuses conducted over the past twenty to twenty-five years reveals that the decline began in 1949–1950 and concerned nearly all species of the migratory woodland birds.

These fluctuations in the bird populations originate from a great many different causes known and unknown, some subtly insinuating, others brutally drastic. Nature never employs just one tool to do its work but like the juggler relishes the interaction of the many. Often a combination of changing conditions explains some of the irregular recoveries and declines that may be noted from year to year more or less consistently. Changes in habitats, the living conditions each species requires to perform its normal functions and live out its normal lifespan, the destruction of many of these through the actions of man, the opening of others accommodating certain birds that can make use of them, are particularly significant. Nesting success, predation, climatic conditions, all these and many more have their figurative finger in the same pie. What happens outside the breeding grounds accounts for the heavy off-season mortality that occurs along the migration routes and on the wintering grounds, hazards that include the increasing use of poison sprays, man's high buildings and protruding towers and contraptions and his artificial and confusing illumination of these, his intolerance and general disrespect for life—all these in addition to natural hazards and catastrophes. Truly, the life of the bird that returns is a charmed one.

The scarcity and the abundance of birds are difficult to determine accurately. The finer fluctuations are easily missed. Here in the north there is the advantage that the birds are dispersed over a much broader landmass and concentrations occur only occasionally. To judge accurately the relative abundance as it varies in time and locality is easier with small numbers of birds than when larger numbers are involved, because in the latter case accurate individual counts are more difficult and the finer nuances in the fluctuations may be lost. One may therefore expect to detect long-range variations in bird populations more readily in these parts than along the crowded migration routes. Uninterrupted observations, recording and breeding censuses over a long period of time in one and the same place are very important. Of course, minor recoveries in certain species may justify hope that the decrease of the bird populations is not quite so bad as it may appear. Also the possibility exists that it may be temporary and that conditions changing from day to day may eventually allow a full recovery. Nevertheless, the slow but steady declines distinctly noticeable in this region, at least, over the past decade and a half should not be lightly dismissed. Here in a few examples are the grounds for this argument.

The least flycatchers never recovered their erstwhile abundance that culminated in 1949. For one thing, the environment began to change so subtly that I hardly realized it. As the trees grew taller, their foliage shaded and closed the light and airy openings in the forest that the flycatchers needed to forage successfully. Later the thinning out of the mature trees over smaller areas here and there, by the wind, natural decay, and man, once again offered patches of more suitable habitats. The flycatchers' slight recovery in 1954 may be attributed to the reopening of such areas, though they never nested again in numbers comparable with those prior to 1949.

The veery was always the most common among the thrushes at Pimisi Bay and the ovenbird the commonest of the warblers. Both belong to the deciduous and mixed woodlands. Both nest on or very near to the ground and like and need good cover. The size of the trees growing in the forest is not of such great importance, provided they do not stand so densely as to smother all undergrowth. Although the open lighter places and the forest edges are of consequence also to them, these two belong to a small number of species that thrive in the closed forest of the north, the thrush in the more humid places and the ovenbird on the drier slopes. Changes in these habitats caused by yearly growth and decay do not therefore affect to any marked degree the movements and the existence of these birds. Until the year 1950 the breeding population of the veery on one hundred acres was about forty pairs and that of the ovenbird until 1949 about thirty-five pairs. The decline occurred quite gradually until in recent years these two birds, once so abundant, have been reduced to no more than ten and fifteen pairs respectively.

The red-eyed vireo, this elegant olive-green bird of the tall trees, shows much the same picture of decline, after having been one of the most abundant species of this region. Traveling along these roads leading through forested areas, I used to be able to count two, three, four singing vireos in every mile. The red-eye is partial to broad-leaved trees wherever they grow—in parks, cities and towns, in woodlots, and in the mixed forest. It likes openings and forest edges and needs an adequate amount of low growth—hazel bushes, soft maples, and other shrubs. At the start of the nesting season the vireo usually suspends its pendulous beautifully constructed nest of birch satin and cobweb at low elevations in shrubs and deciduous trees, more rarely in ever-

greens. But after a failure, with each repeated attempt, it yields to an inclination quite common in many birds to climb successively higher, sometimes into the very tops of the tallest poplars. The decline of the red-eyed vireo began slowly at first in 1950. Thereafter it gathered momentum until of late only about fifteen pairs or less may be found where twenty-five to thirty-five used to nest regularly twenty years ago on a hundred acres of land. With its more specific habitat requirements the red-eyed vireo may be more sensitive than the veery and the ovenbird to slight changes in the woodland environment. But it also figures prominently in the records of tower kills during migration, and, so far as I am aware, very little is known about its resistance to poison sprays.

The population trends of thirteen warblers are similar; only the start of the decline varies slightly, with nearly half of them already showing signs of it in 1947 and the rest over the following years up to 1951. The decline is gradual up to 1956, but after that the number drops sharply in all but the most common, the chestnut-sided warbler, whose population low occurs two years later. In the mourning warbler a definite recovery was noticeable after the 1956 low, but this lasted only two years and then its numbers dwindled again. The redstart also showed a slight recovery after 1956, but this, too, proved to be only temporary. In four—the chestnut-sided, mourning, and Canada warblers, and the yellowthroat—the total decline of each represents a drop of about 70 to 80 percent of their former abundance; in the rest 10 percent or less. The changes wrought in the environment, for the most part natural, should not affect these thirteen warblers to any marked degree. The forest edges still remain much the same, with a few more edges added; the tall evergreens, the myrtle warbler's and Blackburnian warbler's preferred nest trees, are still available in their former abundance and so are the drier parts of the forest floor under the lighter bushes and trees, attractive nesting places for the Nashville, black-and-white, and mourning warblers. Only the chestnut-sided warbler and the redstart might be expected to find the amount of lighter areas insufficient, but judging by the circumstance that their present numbers are about two or three times greater than those of the other warblers, this does not seem to be the ill from which they are suffering.

Changes in the environment of the rose-breasted grosbeak may provide sufficient explanation for its decline since 1947. This lovely bird with the honeyed voice demands a specific kind of nesting accommodation that this land provided perfectly twenty years ago. It likes best to place its nest on the topmost flat circlets of branches of young spruces and balsam firs standing well sheltered in a thicket of deciduous saplings just tall enough to overshadow the site. The nest is built of twigs and rootlets, a transparent, flimsy-looking, but astonishingly durable saucer that remains intact through rains and storms often for more than a year. The disappearance of this kind of habitat does not, however, chase the grosbeak away at once. Individually they are inclined to stick with their original choice of territory to the end of their lives, and in so doing they show no little capacity for adjustment. Under these conditions the grosbeak may place its nest in such unusual spots as the pendant branch of a middle-sized fir or a willow in an alder thicket or even on any suitable flat platform in tall mature birches at three or four times the habitual elevation. Such adaptability on the part of the rose-breasted grosbeak ought to enhance the possibility of its recolonization of our forest, but this has not happened, and after 1956 the population decreased to an all-time low. There is just a chance, if the birds still exist in sufficient numbers, that the severe pulpwood cutting in Green Woods in recent years may help. Here the saw and the ax have thrown open the forest floor to the heavens, causing myriads of poplar seeds to sprout. A young deciduous thicket is now in the making, with a scattering of young evergreens growing up here and there. And who knows but that on a dewy morning in May we shall once again be able to watch the rose-breasted grosbeaks in their black-and-white summer finery, with rosy-red down their fronts and under their wings, performing their courtship displays among our trees!

The sharp decline in the purple finches that began in 1947 masks quite a different set of circumstances. This finch nests in the top of the tall spires of full-grown balsam firs. There is no lack of these, nor is there likely to be unless the whole forest is demolished. The abundance of the species in any given locality is like that of the other finches, tied to the supply of winter foods, buds, frozen wild fruits, and in particular evergreen seeds. Neither a true nomadic species, like the crossbills and the pine siskins that nests wherever a good supply of food is encountered at the right time, nor a true migrant that regularly winters in the south and returns north in spring, purple finches, color-banding proves, tend to be faithful to the place where they first bred and to return to it each year no matter where they spent the winter. Hence the area to which they are attracted by an abundance of food during their first winter and spring may become their home for the rest of their lives. Over a number of years the population of purple finches declines to low levels and then a year comes when a bumper crop of winter foods brings a new influx of young birds to reoccupy the forest and replenish the population. The disaster that took place in the spring of 1956 and affected so many of the other birds probably had little or nothing to do with the decline of the purple finches after that year.

By contrast to the other birds, the white-throated sparrows and the song sparrows present fairly stable population levels with only comparatively minor fluctuations from year to year. In the white-throated, an apparently cyclic tendency creates peaks every fourth or fifth year with corresponding lows that bring its numbers down to about half their peak values. Bird of the great forest, of the tangled underbrush and the dry places, where the scent of sunbaked pine needles fills the air and the blueberries grow luscious and sweet, the white-throated sparrow pops forth from under the brushpile with a disgruntled note, *chunk*. The nest cannot be far away, the alarm of the bird is real, and lest you step on the precious thing snuggled under the blueberry bush, you do best to retire from the scene with the utmost caution. The next moment the bird mounts above the ground-level entanglements into the top of a nearby evergreen, there to enunciate its loud whistled song. The music of the white-throated sparrow is of the very essence of these northern forests, clear and full as the sound of running spring water.

I know of no bird's theme so simply composed that is so exquisitely variable in pitch and intonation. One bird of my acquaintance that lived in the area where the crossbills nested sang with an extra note superimposed into the middle of its song; another never got to the end of the ordinary theme but left off on a note suspended in the middle of it; and many had such consistently different intonations that I could easily distinguish them from the others inhabiting the same neighborhood.

Spring was late in coming in 1956. The ice on the lake broke up and went out on the latest date on record, May 7. The next day was so cold that new ice formed along the shores, just as it does in the fall when the water is about to freeze for the winter. The latter part of April had also been unusually cold with continuing hard frosts almost every night. During the dark hours of the last day of April three inches of snow fell. At dawn the landscape was indescribably beautiful; the sun rose brick-red and tinted the fantastic white lacework of snow with a strong reddish hue outlining every tree, bush, and twig; and the snow pads weighing down the branches of the evergreens glowed in its light. But underneath, buried under the snow, spring stirred, half dormant, rising against the opposing forces of frost and snow.

This kind of weather put the bird migration altogether out of kilter. The few birds that came through into our area, scattered in small advance troops and moving in spite of the weather during those last days of April, were on an average five to eleven days late. Somewhere in the south the great mass of migrants was stalled, held up as by an invisible wall of inclement weather and swelling like water dammed behind an obstruction in the river. And this was the prelude to what came to pass.

On the second day of May, a flow of warm air penetrated into the Pimisi Bay region from the south for a brief few hours before it clashed head on with another advancing mass of polar air. But ere the cold air had time to halt all movement, a small part of the long-awaited stream of accumulated and delayed migrants arrived: robins, flickers, geese, ducks and white-throated sparrows, even a few barn swallows. Soon the swallows, the only ones of the lot subsisting exclusively on insects, were desperately struggling over the ice and what there was of open water hawking for food they must catch to survive. Their inner clocks had urged them to move on and they had obeyed the impulse and run unwittingly into this deadly predicament. A little later I found them perched dismally in a low willow, huddled together to keep warm, inactive and silent.

The wintry weather continued for more than a week and preserved intact the snowdrifts a foot high in the shaded nooks of the forest. Then on May 11 the wind turned south and the temperature rose. Thunderstorms came up accompanied by heavy showers, a weather system in advance of an oncoming heat wave that soon was to engulf a large part of the eastern continent. The next day the temperature reached an improbable 83 degrees in the shade. The buds on the trees began to swell visibly and of a sudden the trembling aspens stood with their crowns veiled in clouds of sheerest light green.

The warm spell lasted three more days, but the expected "wave" of mirgating birds did not materialize. Throughout those three days of warm weather our forest was virtually empty of birds. Where were they? I was not to know until later that the birds were moving all right in an enormous mass, fast, in a great hurry through the air across the Pimisi Bay region, unseen.

In the night of May 15–16 a cold front skimmed ominously out of the Arctic in over the warm air mass, heavy and depressing. It brought freezing temperatures even in the daytime. It covered the ground with snow, and icicles hung from the eaves. There was snow in the mayflowers, snow in the red maple blossoms. And the birds that were going north through the skies on that fatal night came down.

By nine o'clock in the morning a great mass of migrating

[209]

birds overran the whole countryside. They came on this day, not through the trees, but crawling, hopping stiffly from straw to dead leaf, covering the ground with their bodies. They wallowed in the snow looking for food that scarcely was there, or sat cold and shivering, trying to warm their freezing feet in the soft feathers of their bellies.

Thrushes came in great numbers, fawn-colored veeries, silent hermit thrushes in no mood for any characteristic light lift of their rust-red tails. There were gray-cheeked thrushes—never before or since have I seen so many of these rare thrushes that belong to the land from James' Bay to Labrador and are glimpsed only occasionally on their passage through these parts. On this day they came down from the skies in a veritable avalanche. Every small olive-brown thrush that looked like the olive-backed, its near relative that inhabits our forest, proved upon examination to be a gray-cheek.

Ovenbirds walked all over the forest floor and in places sheltered from the snow turned over the dead leaves, one by one, looking for a snail, a mite, whatever edible thing the leaf might cover. Nashville warblers, bright yellow dots in the snow, fed ravenously upon the yellow stamens of the pussy-willows. And least flycatchers, feeling the cold badly with their utter dependence on winged insect life, hopped dismally from one grass-blade to another, close, close to the ground. They were too bone-cold to take any notice of me, stepping cautiously among them lest inadvertently I should trample one underfoot.

At eleven o'clock the birds were still coming on, crawling northward along the ground. They covered the roadsides and the wires of the guide-rails in great numbers, thrushes and more thrushes, white-crowned and white-throated sparrows, rose-breasted grosbeaks.

Down in the marshes close to the surface of the water flocks of birds gathered, attracted by the little bit of warmth that spread into the air from the water and gave life to the smallest of small flying insects. Groups of warblers, buoyed by these gifts of life, flitted about in pursuit of the flies, looking, in their multicolored plumages, like beings misplaced from far different climes. From the reed stalks and any flotsam able to support the light weight, least and alder flycatchers, in perfect amity fostered by the dire emergency, made short sallies into the air, snapping their bills over the minute objects. Seeing them side by side, there was no difficulty in telling these look-alike birds apart by their differences in size and coloring. Small throngs of chipping sparrows in their best spring finery, their reddish hats shining in the dull light, were fly-catching too; they performed the quick twists and turns of this specialized type of food hunting with a dexterity I never expected to see in birds with such short rounded wings.

All through the day the birds moved slowly and laboriously northward across the Pimisi Bay region in the teeth of the piercing wind, hugging the ground, seeking what scant shelter there was to be found from the icy blasts. As night came it grew colder and colder. A ruby-throated hummingbird, rebuffed by the wind, fell on the cold cement foundation of the house and clung there for a long miserable minute, then miraculously found strength to lift upon vibrating wings, hovering along our windows and then disappearing toward the north in the gathering dusk.

It froze hard during the night. As dawn came the flycatchers and the warblers had tracelessly disappeared. The greater mass of these birds that came into this region on that dreadful day, crawling onward dominated by the one urgency to reach their well-known breeding grounds, powered by their last ergon of energy, must have perished.

But the thrushes and the sparrows, hardier than the insect-eaters, survived. They flocked to the feeding station, all but the gray-cheeks which on this second day were replaced by an equally notable influx of olive-backed thrushes. The white-crowned sparrows, proud birds of the far north, interrupted all their activities with song; they sang as they fed greedily on the ground, as they rested, as they preened, as they chased one another through the trees. Having thus come upon the same rigorous conditions they would undoubtedly meet on the tundra, the goal of their journey, perhaps they thrilled to the illusory feeling of having already arrived and expressed it in the most enchanting chorus of haunting plaintive melodies ever heard in these parts.

Ten more days the murderous cold weather persisted. For the small insectivorous birds it was catastrophic. But they continued to come, driven by the irrepressible impulse to go north; and there were so many of them. They came in straggling groups through the days, always traveling close to the ground, never once ascending into the tree tops, their habitual stratum. Low-flying insects grounded the birds more than the cold itself, and judging by the behavior of the crawling birds there were not many of these. At one time I nearly stepped on a tiny orange-crowned warbler sitting huddled by a small tuft of grass. Seen from this unusual angle in its olive-green nuptial plumage with the bright orange crown feathers separated and fully exposed, the very beauty of the bird made it a sight of unforgettable touching pathos.

During these ten fateful days in the late spring of 1956, untold numbers of woodland songbirds must have perished. From around the lakes west of Pismisi Bay reports came of scores of them having been picked up dead from starvation and exposure. In the forest they fell into the leaves as they reached the inevitable end of the journey, upon the beds of green mosses and forest debris. And nature took care of their tiny bodies and buried them, unseen and uncounted.

CHAPTER ELEVEN

The Aftermath

The year after the great disaster I awaited the return of the migrating birds with special interest to see what effects, if any, could justifiably be attributed to the destruction of so many birds.

Natural disasters happen constantly with varying effects upon the living world. But because of life's almost limitless capacity to rebound, the injury and death they cause, although painful enough, are seldom sufficient to bring about radical changes in the average trends of animal populations. However, I did record declines in the numbers of many of the woodland songbirds, especially in the least flycatchers and in almost all of the warblers, too conspicuous to acquit the disaster of all connection. And the fact that these particular species were affected most severely also supported this conclusion.

But, generally speaking, this was not the most important consequence of the disaster. The gradual decline in the numbers of songbirds had hitherto been of vague a character as to be barely noticeable. The marks left by events one year on the general trends in the fluctuations of animal numbers may be erased the next or two years hence, and usually no single circumstance is responsible for whatever changes take place. But since an almost imperceptible decline had been developing over one or two decades, the disaster helped to underline it. The resulting mortality and the failure of the usual recovery to take place afterward were factors tangible enough to focus my attention at last upon what was actually going on. Even so, the signs were far from spectacular. Sometimes it seemed an open question whether or not I was just imagining a meaningful change, a significant displacement of certain species whose disappearance ought to be deplored not only for aesthetic and sentimental but for biological reasons as well. But let the records of my daily observations, continued almost without interruption over the past twenty-five years, be allowed to speak for themselves.

Thirty years ago no noisy outboard motors stirred up swell on Pimisi Bay or up and down the river. The famed portage at Talon Chute with its mighty rocky shelves rising in tiers along the white water of the gorge to the level of Talon Lake, with its blueberry patches full of sweet fruit and its clusters of poison ivy, its velvety dark-green rock mosses and its rare ferns clinging to the crevices in the rock, was then pristine wilderness unsullied by empty cans and abandoned campfires, flattened ground cover and worn paths.

At the break of dawn our red canoe glides silently over the black water with only a rippled wake marking its passage along the river toward the Chute. We move slowly past the undulating formations of this amazing country where one ravine gives way to a rising crest of rock and forest, which in turn gives way to another ravine. A trickling woodland rivulet waters the last ravine and plays soft music as it pours into the deep dark river. Every ravine, every rounded rise of land, is occupied by its own community of birds. Their songs reveal their whereabouts and identify each one.

Strummed from the mysterious green depths, the harp of the unseen hermit thrush strikes its chords in the high register and the lovely melody trails to an end in an almost inaudible pianissimo, delivered with a detachment nothing else upon this earth can imitate. And as we glide past the point where the thrush's song rings loudest and the sound of it grows gradually fainter, we catch the first notes of the next thrush in the adjoining territory intoning its aria while the notes of the first one die away. All along the river the interval separating each singing hermit thrush from the next is seldom wide enough to bring them entirely out of earshot of one another. The olive-backed thrushes are not settled quite so close together as the hermit thrushes. The songs of these two birds are very similar; we listen carefully for the minor differences that distinguish them—the single note with which the hermit thrush introduces its aria, the rolling contralto quality of the olive-back's voice as compared with the coloratura effect of the hermit's delivery.

Hidden among the water-retentive mosses and the trickling streamlets, among the rotting windfalls and the debris deep at the bottom of the ravines, the winter wrens dwell. Nearly every ravine is inhabited by its own perky wren whose rippling series of loudly accented notes sounds ravishingly out over the water; the cliffs embrace each note and add further force to it acoustically. And in every place where there is water we find also a northern waterthrush, especially addicted to small snails found under the dead leaves at the water's edge for its food, and to hideaways under mossy logs or in upturned roots for its nests. A singer of power and repute, this otherwise retiring little brownish-gray bird lets its notes gush forth in a loud ringing cadence, one from over here, and another a bit farther away, and still another a piece up the river.

All along the shores of Pimisi Bay and the Mattawa River we pass from concert to concert. If the thrushes and the wrens and the waterthrushes with their elaborate and striking themes must be considered the star artists of these dawn recitals, doz-

ens of others—warblers, vireos, white-throated sparrows—supply a varied accompaniment; and all of this is occasionally
punctuated by the sustained aria of a purple finch holding forth
from a tree top or by the staccato warble of a song sparrow
almost invisible amid the brownish tints at the water's edge. On
very special occasions and in very special places the strangely
fascinating awakening song of a single wood pewee catches our
delighted ear as it mingles with the rest, this continuous gently
slurred song whose haunting quality transfers it out of the com-
monplace and pulls at the heart-strings as does all good music.

At night the moon is full and its reflected face runs over the
smooth water just ahead of the bow as our canoe rides the current down the river. The ghostly outlines of the shores extend
on both sides, the detailed shapes of their trees and rocks erased
and their shadowy contours melting into the dusky bluish-gray
hues of the night. Before the last of the daylight fades away a
dozen nighthawks on "windowed" wings perform their aerial

acrobatics above us. We watch them making their booming power dives, detached from the earth against the darkening sky, having reached perfection in form and movement as creatures born to speed and aeronautics. Presently the late-evening concert of the thrushes comes to a lingering end and from the larger sections of the land surrounding the bay the whippoorwills begin calling; the water carries the sound of their voices far and wide. The moon rises slowly in the sky and we hardly move. A brooding silence descends upon our magic world; it provides a fitting medium in which the separate sudden outbursts of the night singers resound to best advantage.

These were the unforgettable experiences of twenty to thirty years ago, when the land, not yet too disturbed by man, still retained a part of the original purity and richness of the untouched wilderness. We came upon this scene at the end of an epoch of respite given the land, not on purpose but by chance, after the great ravaging of the virgin forests during the end of the last century and the beginning of this one. Fortuitous as it may have been, this was a blessed interval of some fifty to sixty years that left the second-growth forests to mature in relative peacefulness and the wildlife to re-establish itself in the niches that it had occupied from the end of the last ice age till the coming of the lumbermen.

Despite periodic assaults by the woodcutters and latterly the construction of the new Trans-Canada Highway, at the time of our arrival a state of natural balance was in effect upon this land. By force of circumstances, the woodcutters' work in those days was done in comparative moderation and did not greatly interfere with the balance of nature. The regrowing forest was strong and virile, the number of people living in these parts was insignificant, and their demands upon the natural wealth of these spacious areas were light and strictly limited. More important, the chain saw was not yet in use and the insatiable craving for pulpwood had not yet arisen. Successfully to strike and to preserve a certain level of give-and-take between man and nature within the margins of a properly functioning natural balance is definitely possible, and up to the time of the great industrialization it did occur. There was not too much and not too many of anything. But today the situation is vastly different, and the balance would require a degree of self-discipline and sagacity that is gradually becoming more difficult to achieve under the pernicious pressures created by fast-increasing human numbers.

When a state of balance exists between the living creatures and their environment there is harmony and beauty and a sense of optimum well-being. Birds and beasts occupy all avaliable niches that best fit their ways of life. In good order and without undue delay, replacements take over from those that vanish, for these are always waiting in the wings of the great stage. All benefit by the propitious economy of nature, given such eloquent expression in Lord Shaftesbury's definition of the intrinsic meaning of natural balance: "In nature all is managed for the best with perfect frugality and just reserve, profuse to none, but bountiful to all; never employing on one thing more than enough, but with exact economy retrenching the superfluous, and adding force to what is principal in everything."

Contrastingly harsh and benign is this vast and triumphantly lonely country, the home of the black bear and the sweet-voiced thrushes, where the paths trod by the deer, the wolf, the fox, by the pine marten and the odd fisher still left alive, by the snowshoe hare and the soft padded feet of the bobcat and the lynx were once well worn. Even in our day the scent of the animals clinging tenaciously to the dew-wet ground cover through which they occasionally passed, was sometimes so strong that even I, following along the same trails, could catch a whiff of it and grasp the information it was meant to convey. When the vegetal arrangements answered to the requirements of the birds living and breeding in these latitudes, not a spot was left unutilized. Environment and inhabitants all worked together in close cooperation, keeping the numbers and the needs within the limits of beneficent moderation without curtailing the liberty necessary to promote diversity.

Now, three decades later, the changes wrought by time and new agents, if recognized only superficially and not in depth, might be hardly noticeable. Except for minor areas currently being denuded to satisfy the pulpwood business, the core of the forest still stands maturing and untouched. The beaver, once almost extinct, has now recovered on a grand scale as a result of a period of complete protection. In many places his expertly constructed dams form small lakes and marsh lands, wonderful reservoirs of water protecting the land from uninhibited and devastating run-off. The trees killed by the water in the dammed-up areas become lush habitats for the hole-nesting ducks and woodland birds. Back of the high cliffs along the river the black bear still hibernates in his moss-covered cave. The deer and the large timber wolf are still playing their important roles in the food-chain drama. The fisher, the pine marten, and the lynx still exist, though in such scattered diminishing numbers that their solitude is becoming ruinous to their chances of continued survival.

It is also true that woodland songbirds still inhabit our forest, but their former profusion is no more. Only here and there in little pockets of especially attractive surroundings, where there is water and a thick growth of the forest understory and of trees of varying ages, where the sunshine penetrates through openings in the verdure and the shade is deep and humid among the rotting windfalls, can the sense of former sylvan opulence still be recaptured. So long as the benign spot is left in its wilderness state, untouched and untrodden by too many human feet, the exhilarating interaction of birds and other wildlife and the environment may still be found there, that once made this forest a meaningful exponent of the balanced functions and operations of nature. But although these places alone contain the germ of hope for possible future restoration, not all of them, scattered over this vast land, are now occupied. Here is the emptiness. Here and in all parts of the forest marvelous woodland habitats now lie silent and lifeless each spring after the migration of the birds has come to an end, because not enough of these feathered elves still exist to fill the empty spaces.

Silent spring! Has Rachel Carson's prevision really come true? Let scientific research take care of the complexity of its causes. Here I am dealing only with a trend that in this one region emerges with convincing insistence from the events I have observed and recorded over the past two and a half decades. If by silent spring we mean the stillness that has descended upon the forest where formerly the voices of the woodland birds used to fill the dawn and the morning hours with their continuous and varied chorus, then, indeed, Rachel Carson's silent spring is upon us today, a portentous reality.

The mutual pressure that the members of the same species exercise on one another is a regulatory arrangement of great significance. A good example is to be seen in the five squirrels whose reactions showed the detrimental effects highly intensified nervous tension can have upon behavior. The least flycatchers, crowding into too small an area on the southeastern slope, developed from overly stimulated competition a nervous tension that made them so noisy and irritable, so prone to react without the instinctive discipline they usually possessed, that they produced surviving young from only one observed nest out of ten.

These two are no exceptional examples. Among the woodland songbirds, for instance, broken nests and much lowered rates of breeding success commonly accompany excessive congregation within a limited area. But when the birds are better distributed there is less tension and the ratio of nesting success begins to climb again, compensating for previous losses when their numbers played havoc with their good luck.

The easing of population pressures brings about several interesting changes in the birds' behavior. One of these is the marked effect upon their singing.

Watching a bird as it sings, we easily assume that it sings simply for the pleasure of expressing itself in song; its pose, its movements, its seeming dedication tell us so. And so it does in part, because the consummation of an urge, an impulse, is always pleasurable. This is the way people sing. But aside from expressing feelings of joy or dedication to art or promoting companionship, our singing has no direct biological function, and thereby it differs from the way a bird sings. The song of a bird is too closely linked with the bird's biological functions to be enacted for its own sake alone. And is it not just this elemental motivation that gives to the lovely full notes escaping from their bubbling throats the kind of passion and enthusiasm that enhances them beyond measure?

The song of the bird is primarily a declaration of self: I'm here! It is directed to the world at large, declaring occupation of a piece of land, opposition to intrusions, threat against aggression, willingness to fight, and, after a successful bout, relief from tension. It is also directed to the prospective mate and thus advertises the eligible male. Song is the bird's assertion of presence, possession, and sexual need.

Accordingly, the beginning of the breeding season before the arrival of the female is the period of the bird's most intensive singing. From dawn to dusk on the day before he acquired a mate, a red-eyed vireo sang 22,197 songs, a feat that occupied almost ten out of the fourteen hours he was awake. This is the record of a marathon singer and I mention it only as an example of what a bird can do under the circumstances. After the female arrives the male usually falls silent, because wooing expresses itself in other ways and requires little song. As the eggs appear and incubation gets under way, the pair usually become dedicated to separate duties. Again the male takes up singing and sometimes this song serves as a means of contact between the mates. After the young hatch, other occupations that do not require expression in song take up the bird's time until the brood is fledged; then the demand upon the energy of the parents slackens, and the urge to sing is aroused once again. With the thrushes this is the period of their most beautiful and expansive singing, because nature acting upon the principle of life's continuity keeps the possibility of a renewed reproductive cycle alive by a resurgence of sexual urges, which includes the need of declaration in song. This sexual revival varies in duration and expression from species to species, and in some—the robin, the song sparrow, the white-throated sparrow—leads to another cycle repeated in full.

A sufficiently marked decline in the population eliminates many of the bird's motivations to sing. Living in an environment with few or no close neighbors of its own kind, the bird encounters no rivals to kindle its singing efforts. Nobody whose presence disturbs it threatens to encroach upon its territorial borders. The bird's domain has no other limits than those imposed by its own food requirements and safe nesting opportunities.

This is what happened in our forest after the great disaster, an improbable and strange thing in these forests that resounded with birdsong in former days. The birds are still here but in much diminished numbers. They still sing, but their need for expression in song arises far less frequently than it did two or three decades ago when so many of them established their mosaic patterns of territories, when space was at a premium and competition was strong. But while our spring of today may be silent in comparison with the dawn chorus of other spring season once experienced, at least the silence is not yet total.

Whatever dies and disappears releases new space and opportunity for other forms of life. The altered condition is a great creator and the change a forceful revolution. The causes of any change in the environment are nearly always highly complex and today, as we know only too well, they are to a large extent due to man's ever-increasing demand for more room and resources. Urban spread destroys vast areas of natural habitats; monoculture is devastating to the opportunities of diversity. These circumstances often favor a comparatively small number of species, which sometimes increase beyond the measure compatible with natural balance.

Actually no direct connection was discernible between the gradual decline of the woodland songbirds and the remarkable expansion of certain other kinds of birds in our forest. The decline of the songbirds had its own separate causes, in which these other species that came to inhabit our forest played no part. Nor can it be said that, if the full recovery of the woodland songbirds should come to pass, the existence of these other species that now seem to be replacing them need prove a hindrance.

In 1961 a pair of starlings built their first nest at Pimisi Bay in the abandoned hole of a hairy woodpecker. There these two birds in the company of assorted companions of their own kind held court for the next three nesting seasons. During this period the starlings increased to two and then three pairs which together established a starling residential district in the abandoned woodpecker cavities of the Peninsula.

In this particular area a limiting factor to starling expansion is the lack of open grassy meadowlands with their rich insect life that plays such an important part in the composition of starling baby foods. Whether or not this was the real reason that all the startlings' attempts at usurping occupied woodpecker holes failed is not clear, but the disadvantages of food gathering, starling style, in the Pimisi Bay area may have contributed to the remarkable success of the native hole-nesting inhabitants in defending their home cavities. At any rate, the starlings showed a marked stint of skill and perseverance that was not in character with their usual aggressiveness and cunning; this together with a variety of obstructions—the size of the nest entrance in some cases, the vigilance of the rightful owners in others—worked very well to keep the starlings out of the active woodpecker nests. Eventually a springtime came when the starlings upon arrival only looked into various holes and departed again. And that was how matters stood for two or three years until the highway was widened with a broad strip of right-of-way cleared and seeded with grass and clover. The full effect on the starlings of this metamorphosis still remains to be studied.

The blue jay is another bird that has notably increased over the past decades. Twenty years ago one or two pairs nested in our forest in the summer and hardly more than half a dozen wintered in the area. Nowadays forty to fifty of them commonly converge upon the feeding station during the winter and noisy companies of six to eight families course the forest in the summer after the first broods fledge.

The bright loquacious blue jay with the raucous voice is a character endowed with no small amount of shrewdness and a talent for mimicry that on rare occasions in the spring tempts it to hold forth from under the green pall of drooping balsam branches like a soulful prima donna. Its vocal contribution takes the form of a prolonged aria composed of tender whistled and warbled notes seemingly fetched from the pot-pourri of local birdsongs once heard, remembered, and now delivered as its own; the listener finds it hard to believe that so protracted and sweet a tune can be coming from so implausible a source. I would not accuse the blue jay of being a habitual predator. Rather it is one swayed by opportunity; in the summer when under the stress of bringing up its own brood it yields to the urge of nest-robbing, and occasionally in the winter when food is scarce and a mouse or a shrew scurrying incautiously on top of the snow proves a temptation, it pounces, kills, and feeds. For all its qualities of good looks and intelligence, a high rate of proliferation might easily make the blue jay a problem were it not for the fact that it is a frequent victim of the bird-hunting hawks and its own nest an open invitation to the ravens and the crows. Nature, giving liberally with one hand, never fails to retrench with the other.

The recent extension of the evening grosbeak's range into the eastern part of the continent we have discussed already. Its appearances at Pimisi Bay were altogether sporadic until the early 1960s. Two, sometimes three years in succession it would invade the region in numbers to nest in the widespread forests, then virtually vanish for several years before reappearing in notable numbers. But then the pattern changed, possibly influenced by the sudden increase of feeding stations established in this area that with the distribution of tons of sunflower seeds catered generously to the taste of the lovely yellow birds. With this reliable source of winter support available, the shifting supply of the forests' natural winter foods lost at least part of its former influence on the winter travels of the grosbeaks, and notable numbers of the birds changed their status from off-season wanderers to permanent residents.

Despite being highly vulnerable to nest-robbers, the evening grosbeak, like the robin, with never-failing spirit builds nest upon nest to replace the robbed ones until in the end it usually meets with success. Young birds just out of the nest may be seen from the latter part of June to late August. The number of juveniles in easily distinguishable plumage among the late summer and early fall flocks vouches for an ample production of replacements. The evening grosbeak's partiality for the tender new buds of trees has been held against it. But I have seen no trees or leaf growth impaired by this feeding habit; one might as well reproach the deer and the moose for browsing. Although any of these activities forced to excess by circumstances tends to be devastating, in the case of the evening grosbeak plenty of margin still exists before the relation between this source of food and the numbers of grosbeaks gets out of balance, mainly because tree buds are only a small part of the grosbeaks highly varied diet. Lately they have been exposed to the attention of certain forestry officials, in my view entirely without reason. Let us not carry "management" too far and unjustly judge a fine bird which, though not a songbird in the proper sense, in beauty and merit loses nothing in comparison with the rose-breasted grosbeak and the purple finch.

From the point of view of natural balance, less fortunate population increases have taken place among the blackbirds—the red-wing, the common grackle, and the brown-headed cowbird—which are spreading into the forested areas during the nesting season. Where they formerly provided our sylvan surroundings with only a sparse and contrasting element, now the two first species are to be found in nearly every place where there is water. After the fledging, they overrun the forest in large noisy parties, disturbing the peace, before they resort to the fields in veritable clouds of premigratory concentrations. Instead of the one or two female cowbirds that formerly honored our feeding station with their presence, it is now not unusual to find eight or ten in regular possession of egg-laying territories in the surrounding landscape; there they distribute their oversized proliferous wares for the smaller woodland birds to hatch and to raise. In former days these not altogether unsympathetic parasites could be classed as a moderate natural control and not a serious threat. But today the sight of a full-grown clamorous cowbird fledgling demanding the exclusive attention of a harassed diminutive warbler without a single survivor of its own progeny is not only pathetic but highly alarming in view of the songbirds' declining numbers.

I have often wondered, considering the difference that ignorance would have made—if I had never seen the unassuming elegance of the red-eyed vireo, the vivid guise of the Blackburnian warbler, the redstart's ethereal displays or heard the singing of the veery and the hermit thrush; if I had never known the vast variety of woodland songbirds—might I not have looked quite differently upon these other innocents, the red-wing with its scarlet epaulets, the grackle in its rich iridescence, and even on the cowbird in softest beaver-brown and shiny black? Might I not then have thought them birds of striking beauty and overlooked the stridor of their voices? And having no others to compare them with, would I not then willingly have conceded their roles to be as important as those of any other birds and beasts in nature's scheme of self-preserving balance?

Change and evanescence, constant and continuous! Who am I to protest or to wish it differently? How can I judge which bird, which beast, is best, the worthiest, the blessed? Under any normal and rightly balanced set of circumstances is one more to be encouraged than another, one more deserving of suppression than the next? Who is the good, the bad, the one with claim upon survival more rightful than another's? Are these relationships not all dependent on proportion rather than identity, on the proportion of any creature's numbers, requirements, and activities in relation to all the other life that earth is sheltering in its lap?

A strong and constant awareness is what I would wish for, in order to understand, however falteringly and vaguely, the principles that govern the expressions and the living of every thing. And I would wish to put up safeguards with realism and with wisdom against the heedless and ominous devastation of all those things in which the finer realities of life are deeply hidden, the mighty contours of the natural land, the growing tree, the budding flower, the singing bird, the stalking beast, and then myself, creations of millennia—not for the sake of selfish pseudo-recreation in their midst, relief from man-made sordidness and artificial pressures, not just to gratify the need of mercenary exploitation and vain possession, but to obtain some deeper guiding comprehension of nature's irremissible logic, of the intricacies of all its balanced systems. And I would wish to help create in all of us, creatures of thought and reason, the attitude that would endow us with ability and sense to rediscover and to realize how infinite these systems are and just how tough and how exact a gauge is set by which each part, the largest as the smallest, the highest as the lowest, is made to work in perfect unison.